STAT

SPECIAL TECHNIQUES IN ASSERTIVENESS TRAINING

2nd edition

Melodie Chenevert

STAT

SPECIAL TECHNIQUES IN ASSERTIVENESS TRAINING FOR WOMEN IN THE HEALTH PROFESSIONS

1,8

STAT

SPECIAL TECHNIQUES IN ASSERTIVENESS TRAINING FOR WOMEN IN THE HEALTH PROFESSIONS

MELODIE CHENEVERT, R.N., B.A., M.S.

Nursing Program Coordinator,
Clatsop Community College,
Astoria, Oregon

SECOND EDITION

Illustrated with soft scuptures by the author

The C. V. Mosby Company

ST. LOUIS · TORONTO · LONDON   1983

MOSBY

A TRADITION OF PUBLISHING EXCELLENCE

Editor: Julie Cardamon
Assistant editor: Bess Arends
Manuscript editor: Jeanne L. Heitman
Book design: Nancy Steinmeyer
Cover design: Diane Beasley
Production: Barbara Merritt

Soft sculptures photographed by **Ralph Johnson**

SECOND EDITION

Previous edition copyrighted 1978

Printed in The United States of America

The C.V. Mosby Company
11830 Westline Industrial Drive, St. Louis, Missouri 63141

Library of Congress Cataloging in Publication Data

Chenevert, Melodie, 1941-
    STAT: special techniques in assertiveness training
for women in the health professions.

    Rev. ed. of: Special techniques in assertiveness
training for women in the health professions. 1978.
    Bibliography: p.
    1. Women in medicine—Psychology. 2. Assertiveness
(Psychology) I. Title. [DNLM: 1. Assertiveness.
2. Behavior therapy. 3. Health professions.
4. Women—Psychology. WM 425 C518s]
R692.C43 1983   610.69'6'088042   82-22857
ISBN 0-8016-1135-0

VT/VH/VH 9 8 7 6 5 4 3 2 1   03/C/361

To birds of a feather

Preface

Waiting in the checkout line at the dime store, I noticed a variety of tiny booklets covering everything from astrology to dieting to naming a baby. One of them was titled "How to Be Assertive" and sold for 39 cents or three for a dollar.

Feeling amused and curious, I bought one. It proved to be worth just about what I paid for it. I keep it as a graphic illustration of how a valuable tool can be mistaken for a toy.

For a while assertiveness was a national fad. Many people picked it up, played with it, and then dropped it when it didn't become the quick, easy solution for all their problems as some had promised. When it became obvious that assertiveness took more than a few minutes to master, many lost interest.

If there is one lesson I've learned since *STAT: Special Techniques in Assertiveness Training* was first published, it's that, although assertiveness may be cheap, it's not easy. Mastering assertiveness requires a sizable investment in time and effort. Becoming skilled requires study, practice, experimentation, evaluation, more study, and more practice.

Assertiveness was never meant to be an end in itself. It is a means to an end—a tool. Like all tools, its primary functions are to save time, energy, and money.

A tool used by unskilled hands will produce far different results than will the same tool used by skilled hands. In unskilled hands a hammer is merely a blunt instrument. Anyone can buy a hammer, but not everyone can build a house. So it is with assertiveness.

First attempts to use assertiveness are usually clumsy and may do some damage. Remember that in the process of becoming skilled with any tool, you are bound to suffer some cuts and bruises and a lot of swollen thumbs.

At a conference focusing on ethical considerations, a social worker told of the difficulties that arose after she taught assertiveness skills to clients with terminal illnesses. Although they were often eager learners, these clients had behavior changes that caused disruptions more destructive than anyone ever anticipated. Disturbed and dismayed, she soon abandoned her assertiveness project.

The social worker had severely undestimated the *time* it takes for the newly assertive person to overcome depression, to work through the anger that has accumulated for years, and to become skilled enough to employ assertiveness as a tool instead of a weapon. Unfortunately, dying people don't have this kind of time.

When asked what she hoped to gain from attending an assertiveness workshop, one woman wrote, "After this workshop is over, I hope I leave with the weapon I came for."

Her comment raises important questions. Is assertiveness a weapon or a tool? Is the assertive person armed or equipped?

Tools are constructive implements used to build and repair. When a tool is used for destructive purposes, it ceases to be a tool and becomes a weapon. At this point assertion ends and aggression begins.

Passive people are angry people. They are often initially attracted to assertiveness because of its potential as a weapon. They literally pick up a bit of assertiveness and flail away. In their unskilled hands assertiveness may never be more than a blunt instrument.

By learning to say no, women found they could diminish their depression and discharge their anger. These were monumental gains, and for some they were enough. Others began to see that there was much more to assertiveness than just identifying what they didn't want to do and refusing to do it.

Today women are taking a second or third look at assertiveness and discovering that it has even greater uses as a tool than it did as a weapon. Having used assertiveness skills to free time and energy, they are now investing these commodities in persons and projects of their own choosing.

Women are more goal oriented than ever before. And when it comes to achieving goals, assertiveness has no equal.

As women in the health professions, we have a collective goal. We want to make safe, sane, humane health care available. Assertiveness may be the most powerful tool we have ever had to help us achieve this goal.

For years, students in the health professions have been taught that preserving human dignity and reducing stress are vital components of patient care. Instructors have discussed at length the health care "team" and have directed many health care workers into the multibillion-dollar-a-year industry that sometimes masquerades as a charitable, nonprofit health service.

As practicing health professionals, these persons have learned that the health care team is a myth and that the service provided often ranges from inadequate to abysmal. They have learned that our health care system can compound existing stress and create new stresses of its own. Patients must deal not only with their health problems but with the side effects of a caregiving system that can strip them of everything from their dignity to their life savings.

Within the health care system, women have been the silent majority. Although we account for more than 80 percent of all health care workers, we rarely have anything to say about the patient care policies of our own hospitals. When it comes to city, state, or federal health care policies, we have no voice, no vote.

When feeling angry, discouraged, or depressed about health care conditions, we can easily blame the men who control the system—the politicians, physicians, and administrators. If it were all *their* fault, we then could sit back in righteous indignation. But this mishmash could not exist without our consent. And silence is consent.

The time has come to break the vow of silence, to stand up and say, "This is not the way humans should care for other humans. This is not right. This cannot continue." If you are uncomfortable about speaking up to the doctor and sharing your observations and opinions, you need assertiveness training. If you have never thought it strange that women don't write regularly for medical journals whereas male physicians and administrators write regularly for female health journals, then you need assertiveness training.

Since we are seldom asked to share what we are seeing, thinking, and feeling at the patient's bedside, we can hardly expect an invitation to share on a larger scale. We have to take the initiative. Women have waited long enough for permission to speak up and to share experiences, observations, and insights with the men who regulate and control caregiving systems. Whenever a patient receives less than satisfactory care, speak up. Whenever a patient is treated in an unkind manner, speak up. By failing to speak up, we are condoning current practices.

Students and practitioners need to prepare to challenge physicians, administrators, and other health care authorities to provide a system that is responsive and responsible. This book was written to assist in that preparation—whether it occurs in basic courses, advanced seminars, continuing education workshops, or as a self-help effort. Wishes and good intentions are not enough to achieve optimum health care. Women are going to have to stop dreaming and start doing something to ensure that this type of health care becomes a reality.

Women have a long tradition of being nonassertive, and women health professionals are no exception. As I gathered information for this book, I found it difficult to round up many positive examples in which a professional woman had been successfully assertive. In groups, in private interviews, and on questionnaires, scores of negative experiences and examples tumbled out.

When a woman could recall a positive example, it was obviously so unique and outstanding in her experience that she had savored the event for years and years.

I hope the day is coming when I will write a sequel so loaded with positive examples that I will have to apologize because all the women interviewed will have found it difficult to recall instances in which they did not assert themselves appropriately.

Meanwhile, I would like to thank the many women who shared their experiences with me. Without them this book could not have been written. They join me in the hope that assertiveness may be the answer for women everywhere who want to give without being taken.

I would also like to thank Ralph Johnson and Argus Communications for the splendid photography and the kind permission to use the illustrations beginning Chapters 2 and 4, which had previously been published as posters.

Although the bulk of the first edition remains intact, facts have been updated, new situations and exercises have been added, and some suggestions have been provided for those of you who are trying to teach assertiveness to others.

On the serious side you will find a discussion of the four phases of assertiveness and an expanded bibliography. On the flip side you will find a rather irreverent song: "Battle Hymn of Uppity Nurses."

Some days you need tools. Some days you need weapons. You need your sense of humor every day.

Melodie Chenevert

Contents

STAT

SPECIAL TECHNIQUES IN ASSERTIVENESS TRAINING FOR WOMEN IN THE HEALTH PROFESSIONS

Of chickens and eagles

Group health.

STAT: Special Techniques in Assertiveness Training is a book for women in the health professions: nurses, dietitians, occupational therapists, social workers, x-ray technicians, practical nurses, ward clerks, physical therapists, housekeepers, doctors—anyone female, anyone involved in caring for patients directly or indirectly.

It is a book about learning to be assertive. Learning to stand up for yourself and for your patients. Learning to trust your feelings and respect your opinions. Learning to like yourself.

Although several books are available on assertiveness training, it seems that a group of women as large and as strategically placed as we are should be able to examine assertiveness in light of the special needs our professions place on us.

Women in the health professions have always cared enough, but until now we have never dared enough to stand up for the quality health care our patients deserve. Hundreds of thousands of women are connected with the health care system. What do you think would happen if each of us learned to be assertive? Some think it would be revolutionary. Others think it would be simply revolting.

The question is not "Are you a man or a mouse?" but "Are you a chicken or an eagle?" Before answering that question, read this paraphrase of James Aggrey's "The Parable of the Eagle"*:

> Once upon a time, while walking through the forest, a certain man found a young eagle. He took it home and put it in his barnyard where it soon learned to eat chicken feed and to behave as chickens behave.
>
> One day, a naturalist who was passing by inquired of the owner why it was that an eagle, the king of all birds, should be confined to live in the barnyard with the chickens.
>
> "Since I have given it chicken feed and trained it to be a chicken, it has never learned to fly," replied the owner. "It behaves as chickens behave, so it is no longer an eagle."
>
> "Still," insisted the naturalist, "it has the heart of an eagle and can surely be taught to fly."
>
> After talking it over, the two men agreed to find out whether this was possible. Gently the naturalist took the eagle in his arms and said, "You belong to the sky and not to the earth. Stretch forth your wings and fly."
>
> The eagle, however, was confused; he did not know who he was, and seeing the chickens eating their food, he jumped down to be with them again.
>
> Undismayed, the naturalist took the eagle on the following day, up on the roof of the house, and urged him again, saying, "You are an eagle. Stretch

---

*James, Muriel, and Jongeward, Dorothy: Born to win, Reading, Mass., 1971, Addison-Wesley Publishing Co., Inc., pp. 96-97. (Adapted from Rutherfoord, P., editor: Darkness and light: an anthology of African writing, London, 1958, The Faith Press Ltd.)

forth your wings and fly." But the eagle was afraid of his unknown self and world and jumped down once more for the chicken food.

On the third day the naturalist rose early and took the eagle out of the barnyard to a high mountain. There, he held the king of birds high above him and encouraged him again, saying, "You are an eagle. You belong to the sky as well as to the earth. Stretch forth your wings now, and fly."

The eagle looked around, back towards the barnyard and up to the sky. Still he did not fly. Then the naturalist lifted him straight towards the sun and it happened that the eagle began to tremble, slowly he stretched his wings. At last, with a triumphant cry, he soared away into the heavens.

It may be that the eagle still remembers the chickens with nostalgia; it may even be that he occasionally revisits the barnyard. But as far as anyone knows, he has never returned to lead the life of a chicken. He was an eagle though he had been kept and tamed as a chicken.

According to Webster, eagles are known for their size, strength, gracefulness, keenness of vision, and powers of flight. According to Colonel Sanders, chickens are known for their taste. Which would you rather be?

The happy fact is that you were born an eagle. We were all born eagles. But if we have the birthright of an eagle, why are so many of us chicken?

Somehow, in the process of growing up, we developed a chicken complex. In our homes, schools, and jobs, we have been kept and tamed as chickens. We eat the chicken feed and lay a few eggs, but the question haunts us: "Is this all there is?"

Most of us chose the health professions because we wanted more than just jobs. We wanted to do something "socially significant," we wanted to be "useful," we wanted to "help" others. But now, job frustrations often outweigh job satisfactions. There are so many inequities. Never enough time to do the important things. Responsibilities great, rewards few. When things go well, there is no praise. When things go wrong, everybody is a critic. Personal priorities give way to the demands of countless others.

Assertive behavior may not cure all the ills of the health care system, but it can go a long way in curing the ills of your immediate health care situation. Assertiveness training can give you the skill, courage, and persistence to handle difficult tasks more effectively. You can set your own priorities. You can learn new ways to give and accept praise as well as criticism. You can deal with people who would rob you of your job satisfaction. You can even salvage your sanity.

You may look longingly at the barnyard and wonder why you care so much, why you work so hard, why you can't just be content to eat chicken feed. Why? Because you are an eagle—not a chicken.

Like the eagle, you belong to the sky as well as to the earth. Certainly, there are a lot of menial tasks associated with health care. Down-to-earth things, such as beds to make, bedpans to empty, floors to mop, forms to fill out. Routine things. Necessary things.

Then there are those extraordinary moments when the sky's the limit. Moments when you break through and share intimate thoughts, hopes, and fears with the patient. When you're able to meet high-level needs of the mind, the heart, and the spirit. It is the eagle in you that risks genuine caring, openness, and in-depth involvement with others.

Sometimes it seems women in the health professions are afflicted with a People Pleaser Syndrome. We try to juggle touchy technicians, distraught doctors, arrogant administrators, and all sorts of other peeved personnel. Our motto has been "Peace at any price." Unfortunately, the price has often been poor patient care.

Try to remember that you can please all of the people some of the time and some of the people all of the time, but you can't please all the people all the time. To live with yourself and to be able to stay in the health professions a lifetime, there is only one question you have to answer: **Is what I am doing or about to do in the best interest of my patient?**

If a chicken is diseased or has an open sore—that is, shows any sign of vulnerability—the other chickens will peck it to death. We have a lot of that going on in the health professions today. What a waste of time, energy, and talent!

We squabble over whether a four-year nurse is better than a three-year nurse, is better than a two-year nurse, is better than a one-year nurse. We scramble for status. Is it better to be an occupational therapist or a physical therapist? Who is more important, the housekeeper or the aide? Are doctors better than everyone else?

The question of who is a professional and who is a technician is a visible open sore for many women in the health professions. We each have different jobs to perform. Yet there is really only one job: patient care. The time has come for us to stand together, not for the elevation of our individual professions but for the elevation of patient care.

If there is a distinction to be made, make it between the professional and the amateur. It should not matter whether a person finished high school or finished college. What distinguishes the professional is the ability to do her job with enthusiasm, integrity, skill, grace, and style.

If someone is trying to peck you to death, you can be sure your enemy is not an eagle. At best, it's an old hen or a demented rooster. Your personal and professional lives are filled with turkeys, pigeons, cuckoos, buzzards, ostriches, and albatrosses. *STAT* can help you learn how to deal with all these birds. It can help you claim your birthright and learn how to fly.

Perhaps like the eagle in the story you are confused . . . you do not know who you are ... you tremble ... you are afraid of your unknown self and world. That's not surprising. It is OK to begin slowly. It may take you a year to make it to the flying-chicken level. But from there it's only a short step to becoming a full-fledged eagle. Once you've flown, you can never go back to living the life of a chicken.

It is not a delusion to believe you can fly. It's a delusion to believe you cannot.

Don't be afraid. Come on up. The weather's fine. Stretch forth your wings and fly.

2
Which came first— the chicken or the complex?

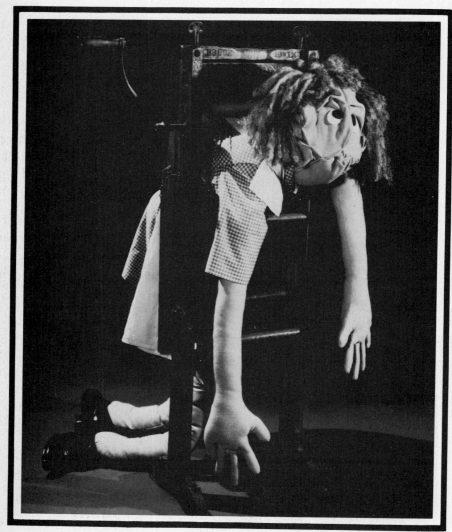

The truth will set you free, but first
it will make you miserable.

Before reading further, take a couple of minutes to complete the following exercise. Get a pencil and paper. Now make a list of all the things you like about yourself. If necessary, scribble your list in the margin of the book, but don't cheat yourself by skipping over this exercise. Ready, set, go.

I have used this exercise with one person and with groups of more than a hundred. The reaction is always the same. Everyone is caught off guard. Usually, it is the first time in their lives they've been asked to prepare such a list. They are startled by their discomfort. Why should it be so difficult to write down their strengths, good qualities, things they admire about themselves? They confide that it would be much easier to list things they do *not* like about themselves. They squirm, sigh, giggle. Most find the task difficult. Some find it impossible. That's a sad commentary on our self-esteem. Sad but understandable.

Throughout our lives, the most important people around us (parents, teachers, pastors) focus on our weaknesses, limitations, sins, and shortcomings. Their myopic vision of us is contagious. Keenly aware that we don't quite measure up, we join them in the futile pursuit of perfection (perfection being a rather fuzzy concept whose meaning shifts capriciously with the whim of the person defining it).

From earliest childhood we try to please, to conform, to mold ourselves into perfection. We are continuously measured for perfection against anybody who happens to be in the vicinity—siblings, neighbors, classmates, friends, parishioners. We jockey for favored positions. We struggle to earn the gold star, trophy, plaque, ribbon, honorable mention. We mimic important people around us, adopt their ideas, ideals, hopes, expectations, and plans as our own. They reward us for doing so.

Herded from kindergarten through college, we quickly learn to outguess instructors. Understanding the subject matter is immaterial as long as we can parrot back the right answers to the right questions. Whether our papers are stamped with A-B-C, 1-2-3, or smiling or frowning faces, we all know the markings reflect how near or far we are from perfection. More important, they tell us whether we are more perfect or less perfect than every other Tom, Dick, or Mary.

This compulsion for ranking and rating ourselves against others stays with us a lifetime. Sometimes consciously, sometimes unconsciously, we categorize the people around us:

	Better than I am	Worse than I am
Brainy	☐	☐
Beautiful	☐	☐
Brawny	☐	☐

	Better than I am	Worse than I am
Talented	☐	☐
Patient	☐	☐
Thrifty	☐	☐
Brave	☐	☐
Clean	☐	☐
Reverent	☐	☐
Other:		
_____	☐	☐
_____	☐	☐
_____	☐	☐
_____	☐	☐
TOTALS	_____	_____

We waste a lot of time mourning our lack of perfection and even more time convincing ourselves that, although we may not be better than everybody, we are definitely better than somebody.

The game of "Contrast and Compare" can be vicious. Even though we know it's ridiculous, we've all been sucked into playing games such as "Perfect Mother" or "Perfect Child." Be honest. You remember how it goes! If your baby weighs 10 pounds, hers weighs 11; if yours is bald, hers has ringlets; if yours can say "da-da," hers recites poetry. Nations go to war with less provocation.

I admit that it's wonderful to be perfect. I was perfect . . . once . . . for 30 seconds.

Unfortunately, there is always someone smarter, someone stronger, prettier, neater, cleaner, wealthier, or braver. Someone to remind us that we are not the best. We are not perfect. Of course, we can always point to someone else who is dumber, weaker, homelier, messier, poorer, or more chicken than we are, but that is small consolation. Knowledge that we are not perfect—and the growing realization that we never will be—can make us miserable.

Lack of perfection might be tolerable. After all, nobody's perfect. What is intolerable is the fear that you are not only imperfect but that deep down you are not even OK. The NOT OK is a crucial dynamic underlying the chicken complex. To understand the NOT OK, some knowledge of transactional analysis may be helpful.

In the best-selling book, *I'm OK—You're OK*, Thomas Harris outlines three life positions open to us as children:

1. I'M NOT OK—YOU'RE OK
2. I'M NOT OK—YOU'RE NOT OK
3. I'M OK—YOU'RE NOT OK

Although the first position is no rose garden, the second and third positions are even less desirable. They are generally reserved for schizophrenics and psychopaths. Some say we are locked into our life position by the time we are two years old. More conservative estimates give us until the age of five.

Once the NOT OK is locked into position, it maintains an iron grip on our lives, influencing our feelings, thoughts, and behaviors. It is so powerful that not even 20, 30, 40, or 50 years of additional life experiences can completely break its hold on us.

The NOT OK is a by-product of having been a child. Every person has to start small. There is no way to avoid it. The NOT OK is the mechanism that can make a grown man suddenly feel two feet tall or reduce a well-educated, competent woman to tears. It is the muffled voice within that reminds us we are not perfect. It is loudest when we are most vulnerable.

Richard Nixon is not the only person haunted by tapes. We are each blackmailed by our own brains. Our heads are stuffed with 12 billion brain cells, and these cells are capable of recording every moment of our lives. The mind functions as an infinite, inexhaustible piece of recording tape. It begins recording even before birth, and everything that is recorded is permanent. Each moment is stored separately, distinctly, complete with all the colors, smells, sights, sounds, people, places, events, and, most important, feelings that were attached to it.

If we could activate the correct brain cell, we could review any given moment in our lives. Think of the possibilities. Perhaps by the time we begin approaching senility, science will have devised a way for us to plug ourselves in and rerun our own memorable moments. That would certainly be more enjoyable than television reruns.

Although no two persons' tapes are exactly alike, there are general categories of information, messages, and impressions that most of us share. These have been designated as the Parent, Adult, and Child. The content of these tapes may be helpful, comforting, unsettling, or devastating. Often their uninvited replay is triggered by circumstances involving tension, criticism, decision making, or crisis. To understand how and why we react to present-day situations as we do, it is important to examine what these tapes have in store for us.

Parent tapes

The Parent tapes are recorded in the first five years of life. They contain everything your parents said or did in your presence: all their instructions, preferences, prejudices, warnings, rules, clichés, mannerisms, and moods.

Because much is recorded before you have any verbal ability, this content is preserved "as is," without benefit of any editing or qualifying explanations. When replayed, these tapes resound as absolute truth from the all-powerful giants who both nurtured and punished you.

These tapes include some essential lifesaving information on handling everything from matches to traffic. They also contain useful information of the how-to-do-it-yourself variety. Some bits of information can become distorted and lead to compulsion or rituals in adult life. An example might be the simple instruction to wash your hands after using the toilet.

A social worker recalled that, when going to the bathroom in the middle of the night as a child, she would be too sleepy to wash her hands and would simply run the water for a moment to appease Mother who might be listening. She laughs when she shares that, 35 years later and living alone, she still catches herself occasionally running water in the middle of the night to placate the gods.

The Parent tapes house all the words like "no," "don't," "never," "never ever," "should," "ought," "remember," and "I told you so." Listen for them in your conversation.

Child tapes

During the first five years of life, the Child tapes are also being recorded. They consist mainly of feelings—gut-level reactions to all the no's, dont's, oh-my-god gasps, sighs, sour looks, shaking heads, and wagging fingers. Like fossils permanently embedded, here are all the fears of being lost, alone, abandoned, rejected, disowned. Here too are lasting imprints of being tiny, tired, frustrated, stupid, helpless, sad, clumsy, inept, and vulnerable.

This is the price of having started life small. This is the inescapable origin of the NOT OK. The instant replay of the Child tapes can make tears sting your eyes or your face flush with shame or guilt at the most inopportune moments.

Because replay can be so painful, there is a strong tendency to lock out the Child tapes. Sadly enough, when you lock out the Child, you also lock out access to the seeds of creativity, because also housed here are all the warm, happy, carefree, joyful, curiosity-tickling experiences, all the "firsts," all the "Aha!" feelings connected with exploration and discovery. What toddler hasn't beamed when he discovered the light switch and momentarily held power over light and darkness?

Adult tapes

At about ten months of age, the Adult begins operating. In contrast to the Parent (taught concept of life) and the Child (felt concept of life), the Adult thinks out its own concept of life. Gathering information through all the senses, the Adult asks questions such as Who? What? Where? When? Why? How? and How much? "How much?" That has to be the least asked question in health care. Even consumers who are avid comparison shoppers for every other product or service rarely inquire about, let alone quibble over, medical costs.

Several years ago when I had to have a vein stripping, I returned to my alma mater in Rochester, Minnesota. An internationally known surgeon at the Mayo Clinic performed the surgery. When the bill came I was amused to see that his charge for operating room time was $6 per minute. I hadn't realized that was how the price was determined.

Out of curiosity I asked my local physician, who had been miffed by my refusal to let him do the surgery, what his fee per minute was in the operating room. His fee was $8. Sometimes the best care actually costs less.

It is also the Adult's responsibility to weigh possible outcomes, estimate the probabilities of success or failure, and then make decisions. For example, most of us jaywalk occasionally. Standing in the middle of the block eyeing the ice cream parlor on the other side of the street, we are strongly tempted to dash straight across (Child). The Parent interrupts, reminding us to cross only at the intersection on the green light (twinge of guilt). The Adult takes over and begins estimating probabilities of such things as our being caught by a policeman (Parent) or of our being run over by a Greyhound bus. After gathering, sorting, and evaluating the information, the Adult decides whether we jaywalk, cross at the intersection, or go home without ice cream.

Another important function of the Adult is to update the information and impressions stored in the Parent and Child, making them relevant and reliable. If the Parent is too threatening or restrictive, the Adult may shy away from correcting those tapes and literally follow in Father's footsteps. The Adult is then said to be *contaminated* by the Parent. If the Parent tapes are incomplete or inaudible, the Adult may be ruled by the Child, and a carefree, impulsive, irresponsible person may be the result.

• • •

When talking with another person (doctor, patient, employer, or spouse), listen for the Parent or Child to intrude. If you have the urge to take over, lecture, scold, threaten, or dictate how things should be, your Parent is in control. On the other hand, if you have the urge to cry, scream, giggle, obey, or hide, your Child is in control. Slips from Adult into Parent or Child are common and normal. Sometimes they are helpful, sometimes harmful. You can develop the sensitivity necessary to assess how appropriate your responses are in each situation.

The mature person has comfortable access to all three and is able to use each component to advantage. The Parent keeps the mind uncluttered by making mundane decisions automatically and supplying useful information. The Child provides the exuberance, humor, and imagination necessary for creative problem solving and innovative living. The Adult continuously gathers, sifts, sorts, and stores information, while determining the present course of action.

For the person struggling with assertiveness, a group experience in transactional analysis may be just as helpful as an assertiveness training group. Assertiveness depends on your ability to stay in the Adult. That means being able to recognize childlike fears, feelings, and fantasies without being intimidated by them. It means remaining flexible and open to new experiences despite a Parent whose replay is rigid, overbearing, and authoritative.

Before a health professional can stay in the Adult, it is usually necessary to grapple with an overdeveloped Parent. Our conversations with patients are riveted with "should," "ought," "no," "don't," "never," and "always." Unless you have a strong Adult, it is difficult to resist the temptation to mother, smother, cajole, or control patients.

If you have kept your pencil and paper handy, test yourself on the following patient situation:

> While working on a hematology floor, you enter Jack Stevens' room and find him packing his suitcase. When you ask him what he's doing, he snaps: "I'm getting the hell out of here! It's been three weeks and a million tests, and they still don't know what's wrong!"

How would you respond? You are standing there face to face, and you would reply, "_____

_____

_____."

If you were in a small group where you *had* to fill in your answer or in which you had to role-play the part of the professional, what thoughts would race through your head? Would you be worried that you would not have the "right" reply? Would you be worried that the group might laugh or frown at your answer? If so, you would be feeling a twinge of the NOT OK.

If you left the reply above blank, you may not have wanted proof of your NOT OK in black and white. Please go back and fill in your own words.

Now look at your response for any intrusion by the Child or Parent. Did you want to make excuses like "I'm only a practical nurse"? Did you literally run away from or sidestep the issue? Is your response stiff or stilted? Did you lecture, argue, or try to verbally coerce him into staying?

Here are some responses that have been given to this situation:

"Just a minute. I'll get some help."

"You shouldn't be so upset. We're doing everything we can."

"I know just how you feel."

"You can't do that!"

"If you leave now, you may never know what's wrong. All those tests will be wasted. After all, the doctor wouldn't have ordered all those tests if he didn't feel they were important."

"I'm going for the doctor. We'll see about this!"

"Relax, everything will look better tomorrow."

"I can't stop you, but just remember, you're leaving against medical advice."

Some lecture, some remain silent, but the majority of those responses are peppered with Parent words, phrases, and mannerisms.

Before responding, it is important to recognize that Mr. Stevens is momentarily controlled by his Child. He is frustrated, frightened, and angry. He wants to run away from the hospital and a dreaded diagnosis. Because he is being "childish," you may automatically slip into the Parent—lecturing, arguing, shaming, threatening. The Parent-Child relationship is scarcely appropriate for parents and their children. When carried over into the professional-patient arena, it can be deadly.

Novels and soap operas feast on the conflict that arises when the patient fails to conform with the doctor's plan. Enter the doctor (Parent Supreme). With righteous indignation, he storms and struts. He lectures, shames, and embarrasses. After his inflamed oration, the patient's eyes are opened. He sees the error of his ways and conforms. The now kindly doctor smiles, and they all live happily ever after.

In real life, however, the outcome is often quite different. The patient may appear to listen and conform, but once out of the doctor's presence, his anger erupts like a volcano. If he is to be treated like a child, he will behave like one. Stubbornly, he may refuse medication, overeat, underexercise, or fail to keep future appointments. He will show the doctor who is in control. Only when he fears death or decay more than the doctor will he humble himself and return. The doctor will shake his head and mutter something about uncooperative patients.

The real life Jack Stevens does not need false reassurance or thinly veiled threats. Since he is being controlled by his Child, it is essential to first speak to that Child:

"It must be very frustrating to go through all those miserable tests and still not know what is happening inside you. You must be frightened.

I can see you're very angry and upset. I would be too if I had spent all this time and seemed to be getting nowhere."

These statements were all the permission he needed to vent his anger and frustration. I allowed him to attack the hospital, the doctor, and me without my becoming defensive or retaliating. After his anger dissipated, the fear began to tumble out. He was afraid he was going to die and we were keeping it from him. Soon his Adult was able to resume control. Together we made a list of all his concerns and questions for the doctor. The misunderstandings were quickly cleared up.

Traces of Parent contamination abound in our health care system. Consider the policies, regulations, and procedures some institutions cling to: keeping vital signs a secret, forcing patients to bathe every morning, making it necessary to sneak children up the back stairs, declining to discuss the cost of care, closing doors when a patient's body is being removed. You can probably add others from your particular health care setting.

My favorite ritual is removing an ambulatory patient from the hospital in a wheelchair. If the patient is unable to make it out of the hospital under his own steam, perhaps he is not ready for discharge. If he is perfectly capable of walking out of the hospital, then this ritual becomes laughable. Sometimes I fantasize wheeling the patient ceremoniously to the curb and dumping him in the gutter. Only a lawyer would claim our responsibility ends there.

Parent-dominated health professionals need to dominate patients. By choosing for patients instead of offering choices, professionals fail to recognize and respect patients as adults and alternately to expect adult behavior from patients. Trapped in a destructive Parent-Child relationship with their patients, they vacillate between duties of nurturing and punishing, depending on whether the patient is being good or naughty. They complain bitterly about patients' draining dependence on them but are intolerant of patients who refuse to surrender their independence. Some of the least helpful professionals are earmarked by their need to always be right or to have the last word. They are overprotective, domineering, rigid, and methodical. They make antiquated customs sacred and threaten anyone who would bring them into question.

As a health professional, you have the right and responsibility to offer patients the benefit of your knowledge and experience—not as a parent figure but as one adult to another. Together as adults you can explore the questions: Who? What? When? Where? Why? How? and How much? The Adult helps the patient to be fully aware of his alternatives, realizing that any final decision belongs to the patient, not to the professional. The Adult can be free to evaluate and alter present customs only when the unquestioned grip of the Parent is broken.

Before you can operate effectively in the Adult, you need to dredge up your Parent and examine its impact on your interpersonal relationships. How do you react to authorities such as teachers, bosses, doctors, or ministers in your own life? Do you tend to become quiet, subdued, obedient, and conforming? Do you find it impossible to talk with them as equals, Adult to Adult? This is part and parcel of the chicken complex: the compulsion to grit your teeth and comply, even when your Adult tells you it is neither useful nor healthy to do so.

To get to the root of the chicken complex, you need to unearth the Child and confront your own NOT OK. When you came into the world, you were naked, small, and helpless. Completely dependent on others to fulfill your needs and desires, you were vulnerable to whatever came your way. You could offer little resistance. As you matured, you became aware of your small stature and powerlessness. You were knee-high without the knowledge, experience, or coordination necessary to fend for yourself, and there was always someone around to remind you of those unhappy facts.

Picture a NOT OK tattooed just above your navel. It becomes a chronic source of embarrassment, and you soon learn that it is customary to conceal it. Over the years, layer by layer, you manage to camouflage your NOT OK. The Parent, Child, and Adult tapes provide partial covering. You gather assorted bits of useful and useless information. You gain experience with all types of people, places, and things. Your coordination improves. (You can even thread a needle!) Shreds of self-confidence accumulate over the sensitive spot. You become taller, stronger, and smarter.

Yet no matter how convincing your exterior looks to others, you are acutely aware of the NOT OK lurking just below the surface. There is constant fear of indecent exposure. That fear propels you to collect other proof that you are really OK. Look! Credit cards, licenses, awards, references, recommendations, publicity, publications, black belts, merit badges, applause, memberships, diamonds, diplomas, degrees! These decorations fill scrapbooks, walls, and wallets with convincing evidence that you are definitely OK. Perhaps the grandest feather in your cap is your professional qualifications.

Then something happens to tear away at your psychological patchwork. Something goes wrong. You are denied a promotion. Your application is rejected. You fail an exam. You dent a fender. You get a divorce. You lose a patient, forget your lines, burn the dinner, sing off key. Everyone has a Watergate.

Loudly, the Child tapes begin to replay familiar strains. Once more you are engulfed by feelings of loss, failure, rejection, shame, frustration, or abandonment. Their intensity has not been muted by time. You wither from the blast as devastated as you mght have been when you were a defenseless child.

A graphic illustration of the NOT OK in action might be borrowed from one of King Nebuchadnezzar's visions. He had many dreams and visions before he finally went stark raving mad and began grazing with the cattle, but this one seems most apropos. In the vision, he sees a magnificent image with a head of gold, breast and arms of silver, belly and thighs of brass, legs of iron, and feet of clay. While watching the image, he sees a stone hurled that strikes the image on its feet. (Where else?) It topples, is smashed into tiny pieces, and is blown away.

The clay feet are symbolic of the NOT OK. They represent any weak spot in your veneer. You may be a magnificent creature, impressively adorned and confident, until a stone strikes. A stone will bounce off places where you are strongest and best protected, but in the right spot it can wreak havoc, leaving you crippled, demoralized, or demolished.

Unfortunately, some people seem to have an uncanny sense of where you are most vulnerable. Children, lovers, bosses, patients, and parents seem to know what to hurl and when to hurl it. Stones come in many shapes and disguises:

> "Why isn't a nice girl like you married?"
> "How could anybody be so stupid?"
> "My mother never made me sort my socks."
> "On you frizzy hair looks good."
> "Just who do you think you are anyway?"
> "Working mothers cause juvenile delinquency."
> "Where were you when I needed you?"
> "After I gave you the best years of my life . . . ."
> "I told you this would happen, didn't I?"
> "Ring around the collar."

Some attacks just ruffle your feathers, whereas others strip you down to goose bumps. Damage depends on the severity of the blast and your ability to endure it. It may take a day, a week, a month, or a year to get your feathers smoothed and your facade properly repaired. Protecting the image becomes paramount.

Early in life, some discover that the best defense is a good offense. It is incredible how offensive people can learn to be. Armed with clubs, they set off into the world intent on smashing your toes before you smash theirs. No holds barred. They lop off toes with tongues sharp as swords, searing wits, leers, sneers, and slurs. All's fair: shaming, blaming, belittling, ignoring. They slap with stereotype, punch with prejudice, and hit hardest when you're tired, overworked, underpayed, and unappreciated. They will try to expose you for what they are—NOT OK.

If you've tried being offensive, you know it's a full-time job. It's exhausting. In addition, it does little to ease personal pain. No matter how many others you manage to topple, your own NOT OK refuses to be silent. Wearily, you may opt for a different protective mechanism that requires less effort and energy. One of the best is distance. Don't let anyone close enough to hurt you. Don't get involved.

Mugged egos are painful. Just as you learn to avoid physical assault by not walking alone at night in rough neighborhoods, you learn to avoid people, places, and situations in which ego attack is likely. For instance, you hesitate to ask a question that might expose your ignorance, or you keep defective merchandise rather than face a cantankerous clerk.

People in the health professions sometimes protect themselves against ego attack by developing a cool, detached, "professional" exterior. Unfortunately, it is impossible to keep your distance and be therapeutically involved at the same time. To be a helping person, you have to risk closeness. One nurse suggested we should get combat pay because our egos are attacked so often.

The universality of the NOT OK should attenuate its impact. I've got a NOT OK, you've got a NOT OK, everybody's got a NOT OK. That puts us all at an equal disadvantage or an equal advantage, depending on whether you're a pessimist or an optimist. Once you can tolerate the thought of your NOT OK being normal, you are well on your way to disarmament. You will have less need to defend your image or to attack the image of others.

At this point, you are entering Harris's fourth position: I'M OK—YOU'RE OK. This position was not available to us as children. It is an elective position that can only be entered into by the adult. It's the choice you make when you agree within yourself to disarm, to be less offensive and less defensive. Only when you accept yourself can you accept others. Only when you love yourself can you love others.

Although you will never be totally immune to ego attacks, you can practice handling them more efficiently. When stones are hurled, instead of crumbling completely, learn to say, "Ouch! That hurts!" You won't have to waste time and energy seeking revenge, slinking off to lick your wounds, or vowing never to get involved again. You won't have to hide or avoid the people and situations that used to make you so uncomfortable.

Being assertive is only possible when you discover you are more than okay, you're OK! The cure for the chicken complex is learning to accept yourself, respect yourself, love yourself, like yourself. OK?

3

Chicks and roosters

You have to kiss a lot of toads
before you find a prince.

Women have some special problems when learning to be assertive, mainly because we happen to live on a planet where men are dominant and women subordinate. If assertive women are not against God's laws, they are certainly against man's.

Male supremacy and female subservience are age-old and worldwide. Anthropologist Marvin Harris says this system was invented partially because of the demands of ancient warfare but, more importantly, as a means "for avoiding the misery and annihilation latent in the reproductive power of the human female." He maintains that male chauvinism is "far from being arbitrary or conspiratorial" and "arose during prehistory to counter a basic threat to human survival—the threat of overpopulation and depletion of resources."*

Ancient warfare required brute force. Since men were usually taller and more muscular, they were trained for hurling and bashing. To make them willing to risk life and limb in battle, the prize offered was sex. Often, only men who had proved themselves as warriors were allowed to marry. A war hero was rewarded with a docile, obedient woman (or docile, obedient women). (Think what a dirty trick it would be to present him with an assertive woman who would tell him to wash his own clothes because she was running for a seat on the tribal council.)

Warfare helped limit population growth, but it was not sufficient. Other methods had to be devised, and the most effective one seemed to be infanticide—especially female infanticide. The normal birthrate is usually 105 boys to 100 girls. Historians note that less than 100 years ago in parts of northern India the ratio was as high as 233 to 100! In some areas of China, female infanticide reached 80 percent.

In fifteenth-century England, most infant deaths were attributed to suffocation caused by a mother rolling over on her infant. Strangely enough, mothers rolled over on daughters more often than on sons. Infanticide was also common in Germany, Italy, and France, giving new meaning to the phrase: "You've come a long way, baby."

Today we have relatively safe and certain ways of limiting population growth. We have the knowledge and technology to help preserve natural resources. Brawn is no longer required for modern warfare. A female finger can push a "destruct" button as effectively as a male finger.

Unless suburbs begin marching on each other, it appears that tribal warfare is on the wane. At least in the United States, aggressive men and passive women have outlived their usefulness. Unfortunately, the prehistoric patterning is so strong that we continue to program our children for these archaic functions.

---

*Harris, Marvin: Why men dominate women, New York Times Magazine, Nov. 13, 1977, pp. 46, 115-123.

Beginning in the newborn nursery when boys are wrapped in blue and girls in pink, parents and society treat the two sexes differently. The physiological differences between boys and girls pale in importance beside the socialization processes they will undergo in the shaping of the adult man and woman.

> What are big boys made of? What are big boys made of? Independence, aggression, competitiveness, leadership, task orientation, outward orientation, assertiveness, innovation, self-discipline, stoicism, activity, objectivity, analytic mindedness, courage, unsentimentality, rationality, confidence, and emotional control.
>
> What are big girls made of? What are big girls made of? Dependence, passivity, fragility, low pain tolerance, nonaggression, noncompetitiveness, inner orientation, interpersonal orientation, empathy, sensitivity, nurturance, subjectivity, intuitiveness, yieldingness, receptivity, inability to risk, emotional liability, supportiveness.*

Our culture has chosen to vigorously enhance certain characteristics in one sex while rigorously inhibiting them in the other. Yet inside every man are the seeds of sensitivity, tenderness, vulnerability, and dependence, and inside every woman are the seeds of independence, competitiveness, rationality, and courage. For a man or a woman to have to deny part of what they are or to pretend to be what they are not is unhealthy both physically and emotionally.

Whereas "all men are created equal," women are still struggling with equal rights issues. Even when legal resolution comes, emotional acceptance of equal rights may be light-years away. Because few people are lukewarm on the subjects of equal rights or women's liberation, it may be dangerous to venture into this area so early. Dangerous but essential. Relationships between the sexes must be explored, no matter how briefly, to be able to understand why assertiveness is so difficult for women.

Basically, women are not programmed to seek success. We are programmed to seek service. "The choices women learn to make are not those leading to occupational and educational advancement."† When women do act in a manner likely to bring achievement, we are accused of being masculine and, therefore, unhealthy. This is the crux of the problem between women and assertiveness. Assertiveness is thought of as a masculine trait.

Matina Horner's work, which seemed to document women's fear of success in competitive academic or occupational situations, has recently been

---

*Gornick, Vivian, and Moran, B.K., editors: Women in sexist society: studies in power and powerlessness, New York, 1971, Basic Books, Inc., Publishers, p. 225.
†Levinson, Richard: Sexism in nursing, Am. J. Nurs. **76:**431, March 1976.

reinterpreted. Her findings may not indicate "fear of success" as much as "fear of sex-role inappropriateness."*

Actually, sex-role appropriateness is one issue women in the health professions can handle fairly easily. We have taken all the sustaining, comforting, supporting, nurturing, service-to-others-not-to-self, approved feminine pursuits and made them legitimate careers. But we do have to wrestle with the conflict between having a career or a family, or a combination of the two.

Columnist Edwin A. Roberts, Jr., writing in the May 2, 1977 issue of the *National Observer,* takes great pains to "defend" the right of women to choose a combination of home and career and then, unblinking, goes on to say, "Fifty percent of all married women in America work outside the home, a statistic that deserves to be placed next to the high rates of divorce and juvenile crime."

Women are frequently scapegoats for society's problems. When we dare step outside rigid sex-approved roles, we are heaped with guilt. Bits of vicious rumor masquerade as scientific fact to frighten us into compliance. Those who are unable to comply because of economic necessity are forced to carry an additional burden.

Separating fact from fantasy about working women is a full-time job. For instance, how many times have you been told that your profession is something "nice to fall back on," with the implication that for women work is just a passing fancy, something to fill time until the right man or the children come along? It is as though all the training, education, and experience you have had is to be used only in case of emergency.

According to Labor Department statistics, however, a woman 25 years old in 1976 will probably work full-time for 34 years, in addition to marrying and having two children. *Thirty-four years.* That's a long time to be stuck in a low-paying job that offers little in the way of security, fringe benefits, promotion, or advancement. If you are single, widowed, or divorced (as 43 percent of the women in this country are), that number jumps to a whopping 41 years.

Although we know that women are not worthless, we are acutely aware that women are worth less in the economic marketplace. Certainly, one index of the relative value of men and women is income. In 1980 women's median income for full-time work was only 60 percent of men's income. A professional woman can expect to earn about two thirds of what her male counterpart earns. And there is evidence that the gap between men's and women's incomes is widening despite affirmative action efforts, because 75 percent of all women are in clerical and service jobs that are described as "low-paying, low-status, and dead-end." According to the U.S. census of 1980, women

---

*Tresemer, David: Fear of success: popular, but unproven, Psychol. Today **7**:82, March 1974.

made up 85 percent of health service workers, 97 percent of all nurses, 97 percent of private household workers, and 80 percent of clerical workers.

Profits and pensions have never had a high priority for women. People come first. Putting people first should not be penalized. "We might say that one of the major issues before us as a human community is the question of how to create a way of life that includes serving others without being subservient."*

Women are people who need people. We value interpersonal relationships above all else and are more likely to consider the needs, opinions, and feelings of others before taking any action. A woman will not think twice about being assertive. She will think 20 times.

Eager to please, a woman is very vulnerable to the You-Can-Be-Perfect-If attack. That's a big IF. For example:

Your husband may say, "You can be a perfect wife IF . . . you sort my socks, balance the budget, always smile, never nag, are superb in both kitchen and bedroom, keep me organized, can BE THERE when I want you, and don't bug me when I'm busy."

Your children may say, "You can be a perfect mother IF . . . you give us freedom, generous allowances, and lots of goodies; keep us entertained; never scream or scold or spank; and can BE THERE when we want you and vanish when we don't."

Your employer may say, "You can be a perfect employee IF . . . you are punctual, hard-working, accept a modest salary, overlook fringe benefits, and can BE THERE at a moment's notice—especially on holidays, weekends, and nights."

Your patient may say, "You can be a perfect therapist IF . . . you are kind and attentive, baby me yet maintain my independence, get me well but don't make me do anything I don't want to do, and above all can BE THERE whenever I want or need you."

Be there. Just be there. It seems like a small enough request, until you consider the number of people who demand first place on your list of priorities.

Throughout life, women are expected to organize their lives around the needs of others. The guiding question for a girl is not "What are you going to make out of your life?" but "Who are you going to make?"

As women, we cling to the belief that our ultimate fulfillment lies in the roles of wife and mother. Perhaps it does. But so does our ultimate frustration. "Mental health statistics have shown that married women are more likely than the unmarried to seek psychiatric help, to attempt suicide, and even if

---

*Miller, Jean Baker: Toward a new psychology of women, Boston, 1976, Beacon Press, p. 71.

non-patients, to report somatic symptoms indicative of psychological distress."*

To stay sane, you need to acknowledge the fact that you cannot be physically and emotionally accessible 24 hours a day without breaking down or wearing out. You also need to recognize that, if you spend the bulk of your life "on call," you will not accomplish much of anything else.

Women spend much of life either waiting for someone or waiting on someone. To fill the time you spend waiting meaningfully, you have to make commitments that many women are reluctant to make. They are afraid to get seriously involved in any activity that might keep them from being there immediately when someone they love wants them.

So instead of filling time, they opt to kill time with a lethal combination of soap operas, coffee klatsches, shopping, or dusting. When the children enter school, and the number of hours to be killed becomes unbearable, women find that skills to fill time have never been fully developed or have rusted beyond recognition. Many women reach their middle years feeling life has somehow passed them by and moaning, "After I gave you the best years of my life. . . ."

Don't give away the best years of your life. It's okay to share them, but don't give them away. If you have already given away the first 40 years of your life, don't let that stop you from planting and harvesting the back 40. Organizations and self-help groups are available to assist you in entering or reentering the job market.

That reentry process would not be so painful or terrifying if, early in life, women learned to spend some time and thought on their own growth and development. Too often, women's priorities are only reflections of the priorities of others. It is easy to rationalize postponing your own needs and goals until your husband gets a degree . . . until he finds a job . . . until the children are in school . . . until the children finish school.

Having someone to lean on has its drawbacks. Women often learn too late that, even within the closest relationships, the only person in the world you can rely on completely is yourself. No matter how much you love the man in your life, you are probably going to outlive him by a decade. It pays to be able to balance the checkbook and change a tire or a fuse.

What has been described as "learned helplessness" in women may be endearing in sweet, young things, but it is tiresome and laughable in middle-aged women. As most women mature, they find it more and more difficult to play the "Poor Little Me/Big Strong You" game. Such a game is degrading and nerve-racking.

---

*Seiden, Anne M.: Overview: research on the psychology of women. II. Women in families, work, psychotherapy, Am. J. Psychiatry **133:**1112, Oct. 1976.

Women must be allowed to openly appreciate and use their intelligence, ability, and creativity. If these qualities continue to be denied or suppressed, Poor Little Me may feign helplessness but take revenge by continually pointing out the flaws, weaknesses, and shortcomings of Big Strong You.

The passive-aggressive, love-hate relationship between men and women has been called the battle of the sexes. This battle is usually fought with cold-war tactics (sometimes bordering on frigid), but when violence erupts, women are no match for men.

When battered wives were making their first headlines in daily newspapers, I was startled by the bulletin board at the entrance to the medical library. Large, bright letters spelled out "SPOUSE ABUSE," and the table beneath the display was heaped with books and copies of journal articles.

My curiosity aroused, I checked the titles of the books. All were about abuse of women. Further intrigued, I took time to sift through the numerous articles. With one small exception, all were about the abuse of women. The only piece I could find to justify the title "Spouse Abuse" was a copy of a brief letter to an editor in which the writer said he had witnessed two cases of husband battering.

The display's title would be justified if nearly equal numbers of men and women were being battered by their spouses. It might even be justified if only 90 percent of the victims were women. But when 99.44 percent of the battered are women, "spouse abuse" becomes a euphemism designed to deny man's abuse and misuse of woman.

The family is not the only battleground for the war between the sexes. The battle is being fought daily at the local hospital. If a picture is worth a thousand words, check the cover on the January 1975 issue of *Medical Dimensions.* Featured are a young doctor and nurse dueling with swords. Between doctors and nurses, the spirit is too often one of conflict and competition instead of cooperation.

When 87 percent of all physicians are men and 97 percent of all nurses are women, it is easy to see why power struggles between health occupations can quickly disintegrate into power struggles between men and women. In all areas of the health care industry, friction between management and labor boils down to friction between men and women.

Most women find it difficult to be assertive with men. Women in the health professions have to learn to be assertive not only with men, but with powerful medicine men.

According to a Department of Health, Education, and Welfare pamphlet, physicians come from affluent backgrounds, make outstanding grades in college, and radiate self-confidence, giving themselves high ratings on a variety of socially desirable attributes ranging from academic ability to originality. In contrast, women in the health professions tend to come from middle and lower socioeconomic levels. They make average grades in college and rate themselves low or modestly in terms of mathematical and mechanical ability, academic ability, leadership, intellectual self-confidence, originality, popularity, and drive to achieve.*

This fragile collective ego not only lets doctors rule the roost in our health care systems, it also allows men to float to the top of professions that are overwhelmingly female.

> Even within the supposedly "female" occupation of nursing, males dominate. Although the number of men in nursing is small, males are disproportionately found in administrative positions. In addition, males are taking over the administration of nursing at an increasing rate. Given these present trends, nursing could evolve into a sex-segregated profession, with men at the top, much as men have become the principals and administrators in the field of elementary education.†

What kind of men go into nursing? Smart ones: ambitious, intelligent, success-oriented men who want to rise rapidly to the top of some profession. They rarely need assertiveness training. In men assertiveness is expected, aggressiveness is accepted.

Pamela F. Cipriano, then president of the National Student Nurses' Association, when discussing "Nurses and Nursing's Issues" in the October 1975 *American Journal of Nursing*, shared this observation:

> At the 1975 NSNA convention 27 percent of our delegates were males. That's a big proportion. We find that women are reluctant to run against them and that usually a male will be elected over a female opponent. That shows how far we still have to go as liberated women.

Because women value men and men devalue women, women also devalue women. Instead of supporting, cheering, and encouraging each other, we are quick to distrust, belittle, and criticize. Conduct your own poll of colleagues. Casually ask whether they prefer male or female patients. Let me know your results. If they coincide with mine, men will be preferred by a wide margin, and the reasons given will give you firsthand knowledge of some women's prejudices against other women.

> Women are said to be more manipulative, devious, inscrutable, and erratic; it has been accurately pointed out that these are characteristics to be expected from any group that has access to power and economic support only by means of pleasing another, dominant group.‡

---

*Trends and career changes of college students in the health fields: a summary report, publ. no. (HRA) 76-54, Washington, D.C., Nov. 1974, Department of Health, Education, and Welfare.
†Levinson, op. cit., p. 431.
‡Seiden, op. cit., p. 1120.

Keeping that quotation in mind, read these two paragraphs from Barbara Edelstein's *The Woman Doctor's Diet for Women*.* In the last section, titled "P.S. What to Do Until the Woman Doctor Comes," Dr. Edelstein writes:

> Chances are that when you are ready to start a diet there will only be a male doctor around to assist you. Is a male doctor better than nothing when it comes to dieting? Absolutely! You will get a physical exam and blood tests. You will get a scale and someone to weigh you; you may or may not get medication and sympathy. You *will* get a great deal of male propaganda.
>
> Let me try to give you a clue about the care and handling of the male doctor who handles your diet. First and foremost—humor him; if you don't feed his ego, he won't diet your body. Second, keep your sense of humor. You'll need it; he may not laugh once during the long weeks of your diet. Follow his rules completely to make sure they don't work, before you try to get him to follow *my* rules. Act as if you thought up a good way to diet all on your own. If you are very clever, you can make it seem like *his* idea, and then you will have no trouble at all.

Women have had to pretend to be less than adequate so men could feel more than adequate. Assertiveness encourages both men and women to meet on common ground: adequacy. Men are OK. Women are OK.

The doctor-nurse game forces women to be manipulative, devious, inscrutable, and erratic. Some persons advocate continuing to play the handmaiden role until physicians are able to accept nurses as independent, assertive, competent colleagues. If nurses decide to keep playing games, they should be warned that the doctors write the rules and women can never be more than pawns. Women health professionals must take the initiative if we want the right to serve others without being subservient. For "even though men are untapped wells of potential, they will not move forward if women continue to subsidize the status quo."†

As long as I can remember, there has been a push to get more men into nursing. Men were supposed to bring stability, status, and higher salaries. Many intelligent women still feel it is vital to recruit men, not recognizing that this is just a variation on an old theme: What every woman needs most is a man.

Instead of pining away, waiting to be rescued, we had better uncover, develop, and mobilize our own resources if we want to save ourselves and our professions. There are no knights in shining armor, and kissing toads will only lead to warts.

---

*Englewood Cliffs, N.J., 1977, Prentice-Hall, Inc.
†Miller, op. cit., p. 76.

4

Ugly ducklings into swans

Destiny may shape our ends,
but we shape our middles.

At the end of our graduate program in psychiatric nursing, the instructors invited us over for dinner. That was a decade ago, and I can't begin to remember what we ate, but I remember what happened after dinner as vividly as if it were yesterday.

About 20 of us were scattered around the living room when one of the instructors suggested we try something new. We formed a circle and then were told to share one thing we liked about ourselves and one thing we liked about the person on our right.

My stomach flip-flopped, and my brain began whizzing wildly in search of something positive I dared say about myself without sounding pompous or obnoxious. I shot a quick glance at the person on my right and was relieved to find someone I liked very much. My eyes scanned the room, pausing momentarily on each other woman, while I fantasized what one thing I would say if she were on my right. For some, a half-dozen good qualities popped into my mind. For others, I was stumped. Suddenly I felt sad that I knew so little about some of my classmates. I regretted the fact that competition between us was often keener than cooperation. I thought it remarkable that I could come so far in life and be more comfortable with criticism than compliments.

As we began to share, there was some squirming and giggling, but, as each person's turn came, there was a breathless silence. All eyes and ears zeroed in on the individual speaker. I wondered if the qualities I had singled out silently would be the ones pronounced aloud.

Those moments were exquisitely painful. I longed to have my turn; yet I was so totally absorbed and fascinated by what was happening inside me and within the group that I savored every moment. The process was as refreshing as a dip in a mountain stream. After the initial shock came intense warmth. As we left that night, I felt we had been given a wonderful farewell gift. It's a gift I would like to pass along to you.

The next time you are with other people, look at them in a different way. Think of what you would say if you had to perform this exercise right then and there. What one thing do you like about yourself that you would be willing to say out loud in front of a group of people? Look at each individual and envision announcing one quality or strength for each of them. Be brave. Actually do this simple exercise at a family dinner, staff meeting, or coffee klatsch. Since most people will be stunned by your suggestion, you will have to take the lead: "One thing I like about myself is _____, and one thing I like about you is _____." You may be surprised at what a difference it can make in your relationships.

To help you get up the nerve to try this out in real life, you may need a boost to your own self-esteem. Take a second look at the list you prepared at the beginning of Chapter 2, when you were asked to list all the things you like about yourself. Look at your list for both quantity and quality. If you are "average," you probably thought of four or five things you like about yourself. Some women can only think of one or two things, whereas a rare bird will list 10 or 12. My all-time champion is a nurse who listed 21 items.

More important than quantity, however, is the quality of items and the tone of wording. Many women wriggle out of complimenting themselves by tacking on parenthetical phrases, as in "a good mother (most of the time but not always)" or "personality (half the time)." There is a strong tendency to qualify every item, thus diminishing its importance, as in "usually kind" or "fairly nice." Along with subtle put-downs are blatantly negative expressions. Two favorites in my collection are "fairly rarely depressed" and "not lame or maimed." Many women write backhanded compliments such as "not ugly" and "not stupid." Why is it so hard for a woman to just say "attractive" and "intelligent"?

Incidentally, "intelligent" is conspicuously absent from the lists I have received. Less than five percent of the respondents list intelligence as one of the things they like about themselves. A television commercial ends with "a mind is a terrible thing to waste." Our minds may not be wasted, but obviously they're often overlooked.

One woman quickly numbered her paper one through five. Next to number one she wrote "honest." The other four numbers she left blank. Apparently, after she had declared herself to be honest, she could not "honestly" list anything else she liked about herself.

Another woman also numbered her paper one through five. Next to each number was a squiggly line or doodle as if she had started to write something but had changed her mind. When she reached number five she wrote, "I'M HAPPY WITH MYSELF!" That's the key: learning to like yourself. If you don't like yourself, you can never master assertiveness.

If you were at a loss for words when you made up your own list, try looking over these words and phrases that have cropped up on lists from other women in the health professions. Circle the ones that apply to you:

Flexible	Honest	Sincere
Loving	Cleanliness	Not judgmental
Capable	Objectiveness	Responsible
Good health	Ability to get along with	Ability to keep a
Well-organized	others and enlist their	confidence
Efficient	help	Big boobs
Good influence on my	Neat	Generous with time or
children	Content	money
Woman	Punctual	Kind
Eyes	Enjoy life	Openness

Not afraid to tackle jobs that are novel and see them through
Initiative
Easy to talk to
I like the way I look
Personality
An easy smile
Reliable
Friendly
Musical talent
Hard worker
Incurable optimist
Good common sense
Weird
Articulate
Good seamstress
Good cook
Slender
Thrifty
Prompt
Do my best
Calm
Intelligent
Ambitious
Good homemaker
Practical
Petite
Confident
Easygoing
Sympathetic
Sensitive
Pleasant
Good speller
Persistent
Craft ability
Loyal
Enthusiastic
Conscientious

Regular exercise
Pride in profession
Natural cheerfulness
Empathy
Great physical endurance
Informed
Fair
Curious
Able to delegate responsibility
Creative
Eager to learn
Trustworthy
Polite
I'm tall
I can forgive easily and not carry a grudge
The age I am in now
Attractive
Emotionally strong
Very perceptive
Capable of talking to groups of people
Particular
Soft-spoken
Good problem solver
Adaptive
Meticulous
Strong religious faith
Great body
Candid
Outgoing
Affectionate
Leader
Altruistic
Curious
Tolerant

Versatile
Thorough
Respectful
I accept people as they are
Satisfied with life
Tidy
Lost 15 pounds
Ability to concentrate
Know myself
Human
Appreciate nature
Not afraid to talk about feelings
Ability to make others comfortable in tense situations
My hair
Good conversationalist
Good listener
Spontaneous
Mature
Straightforward
Insightful
Neurotic
Poised
Ability to laugh
Resourceful
Experienced
Realistic
Fingernails
Good dancer
Giggly
Sweet
Trusting
Witty
Rich
Alive

If you are asked to name something you like about yourself now, you should be more than ready. Try sharing this experience with others close to you. We need all the encouragement we can get to look at ourselves and each other in a positive manner.

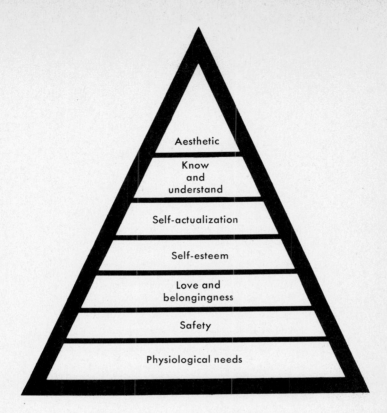

You are probably familiar with Abraham Maslow's hierarchy of human needs.* It has been reproduced innumerable times. Most often it is diagrammed as a pyramid as shown above.

Every time I see this diagram, I am more convinced it should be drawn like an hourglass instead of a pyramid, with a bottleneck at self-esteem as shown on p. 32.

Ugly duckling or swan, chicken or eagle, NOT OK or OK, the crux is self-esteem. Before you can fly, you have to squeeze through that bottleneck. The passage is so difficult that few people negotiate it, and fewer women than men make it.

Women, especially those of us in caring professions, tend to be so other-centered that we often lose touch with ourselves. Our self-esteem is an unstable quality that vacillates depending on the mercy of those around us at any given moment. When questioned about who we are, we look to others for our very definition. Each person we ask—parent, priest, patient, spouse,

*Maslow, Abraham H.: Motivation and personality, ed. 2, New York, 1970, Harper & Row, Publishers, Inc., pp. 35-58.

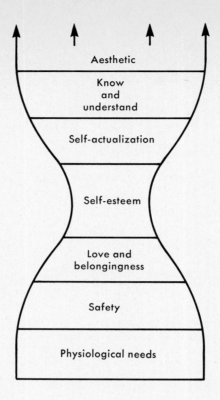

child, teacher, boss, friend, expert—sees us differently. It is like being trapped in a hall of mirrors. Their images of us conflict. Reality or reflection? There is so much distortion in the eye of the beholder it is difficult to tell.

Paralyzed by fear of what others might think if we stop living up to the image, we retreat from the self-esteem conflict back to the lower levels of safety, love, and belongingness. Unfortunately, there is no way to become self-actualizing while keeping one foot firmly planted in the lower levels.

If you wait for someone else to give you permission to move up in the hierarchy, you will remain forever trapped at the bottom of the hourglass. The only person who can give you permission to move is you. Deciding to move upward is a conscious decision. It involves letting go of some excess baggage—anxieties, fears, defenses, excuses, prejudices, clichés, and rituals. It takes guts to break with tradition and status quo, to step away from others who delight in pointing out your flaws and shortcomings, to give up groveling, wallowing in guilt, or mourning your lack of perfection.

Like Alice stepping through the looking glass into Wonderland, you will find your world altered when you dare confront your reflection. New experiences, feelings, and adventures await you. Entrance into the self-actualization level frees you to become all you can be—not just what you think you should be or, more correctly, what you think others think you should be. At last you are free to explore and learn for the sheer joy of it. You have time and energy to develop aesthetic awareness. The sky's the limit.

A major benefit of working your way above the bottleneck is that it is much harder for people and events to get you down. The passage is so narrow that it is hard to slip back into the NOT OK once you've made the climb. To push you down takes a real catastrophe—not just a snide remark or a bit of tension. You find you are stronger, more comfortable with yourself, and less afraid of involvement, caring, and love. All the things you feared you might lose (safety, love, and belonging) are now open to you in an extraordinarily satisfying way.

People trapped in the bottom of the hourglass will try to discourage you. They will play on your fear and ambivalence. They will try to convince you that everything worthwhile is already there at the lower level. They will tell you that upper-level human needs are reserved for the brilliant, the saintly, the rich, or the gifted. In short they will say, "You can't get there from here." Don't you believe it. Watch out for those yellow-bellied sapsuckers. Ignore them and keep going.

Luckily, there are some magic words to help you squeak through the self-esteem bottleneck. They were first uttered by Jesse Lair in the book of the same name: "I ain't much, baby—but I'm all I've got." Those words may be less poetic than "Shazam!," "Open sesame," or "Bibbity bobbity boo," but they are more functional. At last you have the answer for the person who slaps you with the old who-do-you-think-you-are routine: "I ain't much, baby—but I'm all I've got."

Self-esteem should be SELF-esteem. What you think of yourself is much more important than what others think of you. Ugly duckling or swan? You are the only person who can answer. Somewhere along the road to assertiveness lies self-acceptance.

This is it!

This is me!

The only me there'll ever be!

How long has it been since you spent some time with yourself? As women, we funnel most of our time and energy into helping others achieve their goals while we totally neglect our own. We are not even sure we have the right to have goals of our own. We are too busy to indulge our delights and desires. As time goes by, we find it difficult to even remember them. Worst of all, we deny our dreams.

You are a person worth knowing. Find a quiet place, an empty space where you can be alone with yourself. Take time out to rediscover who you are, where you're coming from, and where you would like to go.

Just for fun, try completing the following statements. There are no "wrong" answers if they are *your* answers.

ME!

My favorite color is . . .
My favorite food is . . .
My favorite smell is . . .
My motto is . . .
If I could live anywhere I pleased, I'd be living . . .
My dream job would be . . .
I wish I were bold enough to . . .
Sometimes I wonder if . . .
In five years I want . . .
I laugh when . . .
I feel sad when . . .
I get angry when . . .
I am sorry I never . . .
My home is . . .
My favorite people are listed here with one word that best describes each of
   them:

_____

_____

_____

When I grow up . . .
I love to . . .
My favorite things include . . .
I wish I knew more about . . .
I have never told anyone that . . .
If I were 18 again, I would . . .
I am afraid of . . .
One sure way to lift my spirits is . . .
I am . . .

5
The right wing

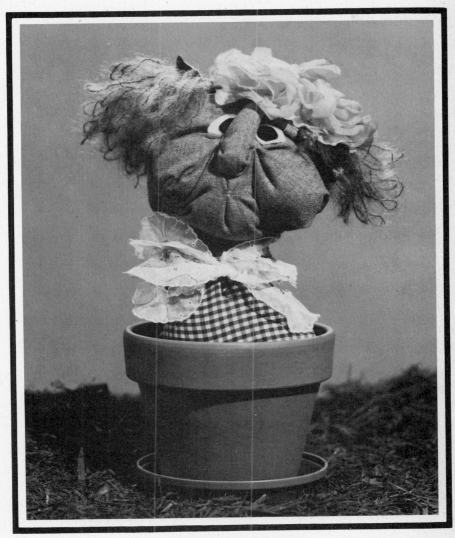

Hold your ground.

Take the average mass murderer. After he is safely in custody, our horrendous legal machinery is set in motion. The process will cost hundreds of thousands of dollars and tie up some of the best legal minds in the country, with appeal after appeal, court after higher court. It will drag on for weeks, months, or even years. No amount of time, energy, or money is too great to spend if we can be 100 percent certain that his rights have been protected.

Take the average woman health professional. It seems no amount of time, energy, or money can convince her that she has rights also. She balks at the mere mention of rights. She has devoted her life to the service of others. Claiming rights for herself seems obscenely selfish.

The whole issue of rights is the biggest stumbling block to assertiveness. However simplistic it may sound, women are preoccupied with responsibilities, not rights. Perhaps the time has come to speak out in favor of a happy medium.

Here are ten basic rights for women in the health professions. If in reading these rights you feel upset or uncomfortable, you may need some remedial work in the earlier chapters. Resistance to rights is inevitably rooted in the NOT OK. It is one hallmark of those trapped below the self-esteem bottleneck.

TEN BASIC RIGHTS FOR WOMEN IN THE HEALTH PROFESSIONS

1. You have the right to be treated with respect.
2. You have the right to a reasonable workload.
3. You have the right to an equitable wage.
4. You have the right to determine your own priorities.
5. You have the right to ask for what you want.
6. You have the right to refuse without making excuses or feeling guilty.
7. You have the right to make mistakes and be responsible for them.
8. You have the right to give and receive information as a professional.
9. You have the right to act in the best interest of the patient.
10. You have the right to be human.

The right to be treated with respect

No one has the "right" to degrade, shame, or humiliate another person in public or in private. And no one has the "responsibility" to sit still and take such abuse. It is time to develop a BM Award (Bad Manners, of course) to be given at moments when words are inadequate to express the proper feeling.

Every woman in the health professions should have a pad of BM stickers to slap on the back of a doctor, head nurse, or instructor who has just embarrassed or belittled her in front of patients or colleagues.

What about doctors who scribble illegible orders and then treat the nurses like imbeciles when the nurses have to track them down for clarification? This appears to be an almost universal complaint from nurses in assertiveness training groups. Illegible handwriting is just another example of bad manners. Stick it to them. Unfortunately, this boring behavior can be life threatening. It should have been nipped in the bud years ago. Physicians who cannot write legibly should be forced to print.

A temper tantrum is a temper tantrum, whether the person involved is a toddler or an eminent brain surgeon. Give the surgeon who throws instruments around the operating room a BM sticker. The rough, the rude, the noisy, the nosey, the bitch, the bully, the gossip, and the grouch—give them all BM stickers.

While we are at it, perhaps each patient should be given a pad of stickers. I am sure they would love to reward their caregivers and visitors properly.

What's in a name? One nurse wrote: "There have been several times when doctors have either called me by my first name—or nothing—or 'Hey you.' I wish I would have enough 'guts' to call them by their first names."

Her comment reminds me of a lovely, romantic, first-person story published in *Reader's Digest.* It was written by a nurse who had been horribly disfigured in an automobile accident. As a result of the accident she lost her unborn child, and later her husband divorced her. Over the years she had much reconstructive surgery performed by a particular plastic surgeon. Later they worked together professionally. Eventually, he asked her to marry him. Even when he proposed, she couldn't bring herself to use his first name!

Although *Good Housekeeping* may not be any more respected than *Reader's Digest* as a source authority in professional circles, it did publish the results of a fascinating poll conducted by Dr. Jonathan Freedman, professor of psychology at Columbia University. The article titled "What Nurses Think of Doctors . . . and Vice Versa" appeared in the April 1979 issue and summarized results from questionnaires completed by 2,000 doctors, 2,000 nurses, and 2,000 patients.

One of the most interesting findings was that, although nurses found doctors difficult to work with, 85 percent said they respected doctors. Doctors, on the other hand, reported they found nurses easy to work with, and 87 percent said they *did not* respect nurses.

Isn't that what our mothers always told us? Men don't respect women who are easy.

In some instances when women fail to be assertive, they find themselves endangered physically.

"In my last nursing job I was exposed to a fairly high amount of radiation. I was aware of the exposure on accepting the job, but I should have been much more assertive about the amount I would accept and the precautions the hospital took to protect its personnel."

Basically, we are trusting. We expect some authority to be looking out for our well-being. Respect yourself. Look out for yourself. Ignorance is not bliss. It's dangerous. Be knowledgeable first. Don't rely on others' authority. Get facts straight.

Respect yourself enough to speak up. By brooding in silence, we make mountains out of molehills.

"As part of an orientation plan in a smaller hospital, I was told by the director of patient services to work a few times on each shift on both the medical and surgical floors. While I was setting up the schedule with one of the head nurses, she commented: 'I don't know why you are being oriented to this floor. We have more help than we need now.' Apparently there was a lack of communication somewhere, but I continued to have an 'unwanted and outsider' feeling. I wish I could have had a proper yet respectful reply."

The assertive response is simply to put into words what you are thinking and feeling. For instance: "There seems to be some lack of communication here. The director just wants me to get acquainted with both the medical and surgical floors. I feel rather awkward and unwanted." The head nurse was probably unaware of the impact of her words. Getting your feelings out in the open saves a lot of misery and misunderstanding. You will most likely get an apology.

"Whenever I start work in a new hospital, I'm always a little quiet. People have mistaken this for lack of intelligence or being stuck-up — of which neither is true. Consequently, I get stuck with all the work, all the shifts, and all the extra duty. Being a newlywed, my husband didn't appreciate it, and he is the one who finally forced me to stand up to my superior for equal time off with my co-workers. It is difficult for me to speak with superiors — nursing directors, doctors, and others."

Pick up on the word "superiors." If you feel "inferior" to others, it is impossible to assert yourself.

According to an HEW report titled "Trends and Career Changes of College Students in the Health Fields,"* medical and dental students come from affluent backgrounds, are academically superior, and "think highly of themselves." On the other hand, nurses and lab technicians come from poorer

---

*Publ. no. (HRA) 76-54, Washington, D.C., Nov. 1974, Department of Health, Education, and Welfare.

economic backgrounds and "have low self-regard for their intellectual qualities."

Overemphasis on educational background is a real sore spot among women in the health professions. Intellectually, we know that there are some grossly incompetent people with PhD's and some incredibly competent people who never finished high school. Emotionally, however, many of us are intimidated by degrees or lack of them. Let's begin to give each other credit, not only for educational background or rank or salary, but for ability to perform well on the job, integrity, tact, skill, dedication, and compassion. The most important things in life aren't reflected in college degrees.

The right to a reasonable workload

When Cynthia Knox (not her real name) first took the clinical nurse specialist position at a metropolitan children's hospital, she was excited by the challenges and possibilities. The job description read like a dream. Who could have known the dream would soon prove to be a nightmare?

Her primary responsibilities were to teach, counsel, and guide the staff along with the children and their parents. She was to develop research proposals as well as aid in ongoing research. She was to help design the ideal children's unit, working closely with the architects, since construction was scheduled to begin within the year.

The new unit was desperately needed. Hers was always overcrowded. Too many children, too few nurses. Soon she found herself working nights, weekends, and occasionally double shifts. Having worked as a missionary in an underdeveloped country, she was not averse to hard work. She was highly skilled, efficient, and compassionate. She poured body and soul into work. Her time and energy were sapped just by the physical care of the children. There was little left over for counseling, teaching, planning, or research.

Exhausted, she went to the administration, which sympathized and promised to ease the situation. No help materialized. In desperation, she threatened to resign. The administration countered with: "It is bad enough now. Think what will happen if you leave, too. Who will care for the children?" That kept her in line for a few extra months.

After almost two years of back-breaking, heartbreaking work, she resigned. Broken in spirit, humiliated, and guilt-ridden, she found refuge in a small, private school where she teaches pediatric nursing.

The Cynthia Knox situation is not uncommon. A major complaint of women in the health professions is overwork. We leap into our careers brimming with enthusiasm and burn out before the year is up.

Some of us flee from our professions physically. I found one social worker selling clothing at a local department store. She could no longer cope with the stupendous responsibility and the skimpy support. The harsh realities of the health care system force many of us to hide out in schools and universities where we can busy ourselves with the intellectual pursuit of the ideal. Housewives once trained in the health professions are reluctant to return to their careers, even when able, because the rewards are so few and the sacrifices so great.

Some of us flee from our professions emotionally. We all know professional zombies who burned out years ago but continue to work in the health professions. You can recognize them by their dull eyes, mechanized routines, lack of involvement, and refusal to question the status quo. Their bodies are warm, but their hearts are cold, and their minds are frozen.

The system may be at fault for much of the overwork, but part of the problem we bring on ourselves. Inability to delegate responsibility ties many women up in knots.

> "When working in a small general hospital, I found it easier to do things myself than to make sure the staff got them done and done right."

or:

> "When I was a head nurse I found it very difficult to say no to requests for special hours, and I would work shifts that were short of help. I ended up with bad effects on my physical and mental health. I do not like to offend anybody."

Another problem contributing to unreasonable workloads is the inability to reprimand or fire workers who are not doing their share.

> "It is difficult for me to reprimand a worker in my charge whom I think is not doing her work satisfactorily. This is something I really need help with now in my position as a nursing supervisor. I have difficulty asserting myself as an authority when criticism is involved."

This nurse echoes the dilemma of the nurse who does not like to offend anybody. We have all covered for fellow workers. We can do our work and theirs too for a short time. If the problem is chronic, however, anger and resentment are inevitable. Morale slips. The patients suffer.

When it comes to reprimanding a worker or firing her, the guiding question has to be: **Is what I am doing or about to do in the best interest of the patient?** This question may help break the hold of the "Mother Hen Superior" complex. We cannot take care of everyone. Our prime responsibility is to care for patients. Anything or anyone interfering with that responsibility has to go.

Here is another situation to consider:

"My problem is my nursing supervisor. I am a shy, happy-go-lucky person but efficient and dependable. For this reason, I am literally pushed around from one department to another, with no consideration for my convenience, fears, or discomfort at having to work in unfamiliar departments. The supervisor's only concern is filling the vacancy so she will look good. She cares nothing about the cost to me.

When I once mentioned I thought I should be compensated for this, I was given a strong put-down. I work part-time for a large clinic as a relief nurse. From my viewpoint, I am cheap labor (I get no benefits). How I would love to go higher up and speak my mind, but I am not assertive or articulate enough to do this."

The first sentence is the tip-off. Instead of blaming the supervisor or the system, there must come an honest owning up: "My problem is me." As any assertive woman will tell you, *once* is not enough. Get one-paragraph references about your work from each department. Approach your supervisor again. If she fails to respond, go to her supervisor. If they do not improve your situation or compensate you adequately, quit. Or settle down to work in a less than perfect situation knowing that you have done your best.

The sad part of many inequitable situations is that, if you quit, they will just bring in another nurse and treat her the same way. When she refuses to be exploited, another nurse will come along. The clinic cannot lose. They have an overready supply of cheap labor. The patients are the losers. What are we going to do about it?

The right to an equitable wage

Does it take more knowledge and skill to be a nurse or to be a parking lot attendant? According to the Department of Labor's *Dictionary of Occupational Titles*, the two jobs are equally complex. In "You Really *Are* Underpaid" (*RN*, May 1979), Vincent O'Neal writes that the dictionary "rates the complexity of the nursing profession on a level with that of parking lot attendants, dog pound attendants and mud mixers."

Incidently, this dictionary is the world's most widely used tool for setting wages, which helps explain why nurses' salaries are so notoriously low. For those of us in nursing education, it helps explain why counselors continue to recommend nursing as a career for students who are physically, mentally, and emotionally handicapped. They obviously think anyone with a warm heart, good intentions, and a driver's license can be a nurse . . . or a parking lot attendant. Take your pick.

The O'Neal article goes on to summarize a study conducted in Washington state where 50,000 state employees including 6,000 nurses had their jobs analyzed by a complicated system of points given for each aspect such as skills needed, education required, and decisions made. Nurses needed 385 points, for which they received a median salary of $13,800.

These numbers are meaningless until compared with other job groups. For example, safety inspectors (mainly men) needed 344 points (9 percent fewer), for which they received a median salary of $19,000. The typical male job paying $13,800 was utility worker II with 138 points (64 percent fewer). To sum it up, the nurse's job was found comparable to a midlevel professional, whereas her pay was the same as that of a maintenance man.

At this time, many of us are left out in the cold. When we try to be accepted as professionals, we are given the cold shoulder by academicians and physicians. We have no status to sustain our egos. To add insult to injury, we are also denied the cold, hard cash of the skilled and semiskilled workers. We have no money to sustain our egos. We have no money to sustain us, period.

Women in the health professions find it difficult to speak of money. Somehow filthy lucre doesn't quite mesh with our missionary zeal. One woman "confessed" that she had returned to work only because she needed the money. She was very embarrassed because she had no loftier goal.

The inequities between salaries for men and women have been widely publicized. In the autumn of 1977, a survey was released showing that congressmen paid their top male staffers 18 to 129 percent more than they paid female staffers with the same job titles. The House Commission on Administrative Review found that male administrative assistants made an average of $39,000, but female administrative assistants averaged only $17,000. Male legislative assistants averaged $20,000, but women averaged $17,000. Male press aides made $20,000, but women made $17,000. By very act of Congress, such discrimination is against the law in private industry. It's the old do-as-I-say-not-as-I-do routine.

A friend in Chicago who just completed a PhD degree was feeling a little low. It seems the pop truck drivers had been on strike, making it impossible to return pop bottles to the grocery stores. As part of the settlement, the drivers received a $24,000 salary.

One weak ploy has been to ask, "Yes, but would you want to be a pop truck driver?" For $24,000, I would consider it. (Why doesn't anyone ever ask, "Yes, but would you want to be a nurse?") I think it's time to band together and demand wages that reflect our education, experience, and level of responsibility.

When I graduated from high school, there were basically two career choices for women: teaching and nursing. From a financial standpoint, it appears I chose the wrong one.

In 1978 I first became aware of sizable differences between average teacher's and nurse's salaries in Washington State where I was living. The gap was running about $3,500 in favor of the teachers even without accounting for the fact that teachers only work nine months of the year.

After moving to Oregon in the spring of 1982, I noticed a newspaper headline declaring the average teacher's salary in this state to be $20,305. I called the Oregon Nurses Association to find out what the average nurse in Oregon is paid. They told me there are no "average" nurses in Oregon. At least there is no average salary statistic readily available because each hospital, institution, clinic, and office is free to set its own wage.

The ONA did give me the hourly average for nurses in Portland: $8.79 per hour. At that rate the nurse would earn $70.32 per day. If contracted for nine months (180 days), the nurse would earn $12,657.60.

Compare that with the average teacher's salary in Portland: $21,493. The difference between the two is a staggering $8,835.40.

Why shouldn't teachers be paid more? After all, they don't get to work on Christmas, Thanksgiving, or Easter. They have to take every weekend off. Few get to work in the summer. Worst of all they are stuck in daytime jobs and miss the fun of rotating hours and double shifts.

The salary differences absolutely defy the laws of supply and demand. When a teacher resigns or retires, hundreds of applicants line up at the schoolhouse door. When a nurse resigns or retires, no one is waiting at the hospital door. It may take weeks or months to find a replacement. Nurses should be worth their weight in gold, whereas teachers should be a dime a dozen. Evidently, nurses still have a lot to learn from teachers.

What about garbage collectors, steelworkers, and automobile mechanics? How do their salaries, fringe benefits, and working conditions compare with yours? Don't forget to take into account inconvenient shifts, life-and-death responsibilities, vacation and holiday time, pensions, profit sharing, and other fringe benefits as well as salary. You can check out the information for your locality by calling your state employment agency.

Our local newspaper ran a feature article on people in medicine in February 1977. The writer interviewed a doctor, a nurse, and a security man. The salaries for the nurse and the security man were detailed, but the doctor refused to give that information because "like most physicians he is sensitive about revealing his income."

The nurse, after 14 years of experience, was making $4.50 per hour working for the Planned Parenthood Association. She recently had left a job working with high-risk newborns where she made almost $5 per hour but was required to work rotating shifts, holidays, and weekends. Compare her salary with that of a checkout girl in a unionized supermarket making $7 per hour. Something is wrong.

"Yes, but would you want to be a checkout girl?"

Frankly, I would probably feel guilty letting my education and experience go to waste. I am not suggesting that women health professionals are worth more than supermarket clerks, mechanics, or factory workers. I do think we are worth as much.

The right to determine your own priorities

Whether on the job or in your personal life, you have the right to decide what your priorities are. You have the right to choose the ways in which you spend your time and energy. If you waver, a host of other people will be happy to make the choices for you.

> "Because I take a commitment seriously, I was careful to attend all meetings of our United Way last summer. I completed my responsibility, and at that point I was pressured to become the secretary, because to them I seemed very interested because of my regular attendance at meetings. I was successfully assertive and refused the position, because I feel my place is at home during the hours right after school. It was difficult for me to be assertive, but I felt satisfaction afterward."

As women, we are receptive and responsive to the needs and desires of those around us. This is both an asset and a liability. After finally getting her sixth child off to school, one woman was delighted to learn that she had been accepted into graduate school. A week later, she sadly reported that her husband had vetoed her returning to school because it might interfere with *his* plans. As women, we should be entitled to some dreams and plans of our own. If you really want to return to school or to work, your needs and desires should have equal consideration.

It's difficult to give patients top priority with all the minor interruptions we have to deal with daily.

> "A patient was crying. When I asked her what the problem was, she said nothing. Again I questioned her, and she pushed me away. I was then called to the phone and detained 20 minutes. I wasn't able to follow through on her problem. I wish I had had someone else take the phone call and tried to determine her problem with another approach."

Electing to stay with a patient who needs you may well mean refusing or delaying other tasks. Women in the health professions are still trying to be in two (or more) places at once. We tend to give in and do things to please parent figures—completing paperwork, assisting physicians, and so on—rather than helping patients.

"Five years ago, I discovered a lump in my breast and consulted an excellent surgeon. He and I agreed it should be biopsied, although he said he was 90 percent sure it was benign. I told him at the time I would sign a consent form for the biopsy only. If it were malignant, I would make a decision only when I knew what the alternatives were.

I think he felt that I was questioning his ability. I wasn't. I felt that I needed more time to prepare myself and my family for the more serious and debilitating surgical procedure. After some convincing arguing, he agreed to do the biopsy only and let me make the decisions that I felt were mine to make. Fortunately, the biopsy was benign. Despite the disagreement, we are friendly when we meet."

It is important to have some control over your job, your time, your body, your life. Be able to say to yourself: "This is right for me. This is right for me now." Life is ever changing. Be brave enough to change with it.

The right to ask for what you want

Although there can be no guarantee that you will get what you want, you certainly have the right to ask for it. Whether you crave a night on the town, help with a new procedure, some time alone, or a specific patient assignment, wishes must be put into words before they can come true. Women often keep silent, thinking others should sense what they want or need. It is disappointing how few mind readers there are in the world.

Suffering in silence can be hazardous to your health.

"About 20 people were crammed into a small conference room when one woman began to smoke. The smoke was particularly irritating to me. I wish I would have asked the woman to stop — I didn't."

Why do nonsmokers still find it so difficult to ask smokers to refrain from smoking? The evidence that cigarette smoke is harmful to nonsmokers is very convincing. Even armed with this knowledge, we are still reluctant to infringe on another's rights. Before you get angry enough to douse someone with a bucket of water, simply express the fact that smoke really bothers you. Most smokers will be polite enough to stop, if they are asked openly and politely. If they don't, present them with one of your BM stickers.

During job interviews, you may be asked to temporarily accept an assignment other than the one you have requested. One nurse who wanted to work in a coronary care unit was "temporarily" shunted to an orthopedic unit. Six months later she was still in orthopedics and angry to learn that two new nurses had been placed in the coronary care unit during that time. The moral is to keep your requests visible. Out of sight, out of mind. Make sure you check in with the nursing director every few weeks to see if there is an open-ing on your desired unit.

Here is another good example of asking for what you want:

> "Our recently handicapped child attends a therapy session established to last one hour. However, the therapist was always late and frequently dismissed the child early. Questioning these shortened sessions, I was told that there was no financial loss since insurance pays the bill. I reminded the individual that indirectly I was paying and, to be truthful, she wasn't giving of her skill in a complete and honest manner. Because I respected her abilities and did not display hostility, we are both comfortable in meeting now, and our child is get-ting proper therapy."

Don't pout or fume silently. Speak up quickly, calmly, honestly. It's your right.

The right to refuse without making excuses or feeling guilty

Refusing to collect for a charity when an anonymous telephone solicitor asks you to is a relatively easy task. It is difficult to refuse a request from a friend or co-worker and even more difficult to refuse a request from a super-visor.

One nurse shared her exasperation at always being called in on her day off. We role-played the situation, and the next time her head nurse phoned, this is what happened:

> "I wondered if you could come in and work on Friday. It looks like we'll be short-handed again."
> "This is the third time this month I have been called to come in on my day off. I will not be able to work this Friday."
> "Oh . . . do you have special plans?"
> "No, but I need a break from work. I plan to take my day off."
> "But who will I get to help out if you won't come in to work?"
> "I don't know. I am sure it is difficult for you."
> "Yes, it is! We are always short of help. I know we need to hire another nurse, but it just isn't in the budget. Are you sure you can't come in on Friday?"
> "I'm sure."
> "Who can I get to cover?"
> "I don't know."
> "Oh, well . . . I can probably find somebody. I'll see you later."

The nurse felt very good after this exchange. No lying, no lame excuses, no ulcer attack, no migraine headache. Most women are more than willing to help out in a pinch, but many report being constantly taken advantage of and then being made to feel guilty and selfish when they begin to refuse.

Giving questionable dosages of medication is a frequent problem brought out in assertiveness training groups.

"I refused to give a medication ordered, because I felt the dosage was excessive. This put me in line for great verbal abuse by the doctor. Although somewhat intimidated, I said if he insisted on that dosage then he would have to administer it himself, since I refused. He finally wrote an order for a more reasonable dosage. Although I had visions of a lot of repercussions, it actually made for more mutual respect. I have never forgotten that situation."

Here is a similar situation that went unresolved:

"A general practitioner who limited practice to psychiatry habitually prescribed large dosages of medications for his patients. On one occasion, he ordered medications that I knew should not be given together. I questioned whether he wanted them both given and he answered 'yes.' Instead of administering the medication, I wish I had refused to do so. This doctor would never admit his own fallibility. If questioned, he would never change his mind. However, a day or two later, he would change his orders."

Many women health professionals have real problems with authority figures. Even though our own education, experience, and judgment run contrary to what we see the authority doing or saying, we are still reluctant to openly oppose or question what is happening. In any of these situations, ask yourself, **"Is what I am doing or about to do in the best interest of the patient?"** That should give you the needed courage to lay your ego on the line.

A clinical psychologist was asked to participate in a panel discussion on women and mental health. The selection committee had suddenly realized they had an all-male panel and, given the topic, it would probably be wise to include a woman. With only two days to prepare and a three-hour drive to consider, the psychologist declined. Earlier in her career, she said, she would have jumped at the chance, because she would have been so flattered to have been invited. Now she found she was comfortable enough with her ability and worth to decline the invitation.

Last but not least, you also have the right to refuse to be assertive. When you choose not to assert yourself, you need offer no excuses or explanations. You have the right to refuse.

The right to make mistakes and be responsible for them

Women health professionals seem almost terrified of making mistakes. No amount of education or experience seems to override the NOT OK fear of being wrong. This unreasonable fear prevents us from questioning authorities, speaking up, or stepping in on behalf of the patient.

Penalties for minor errors on the job can be so ego shattering that many women are afraid to admit mistakes. Fully conscious that human lives are involved, we agree that there is no room for error. But everyone makes mistakes—the most skillful surgeon and the least skillful nurse's aide. Never being wrong should not be more important than doing right. Maintaining an infallible image is never in the patient's best interest.

An occupational therapist came upon a man who had had a heart attack. Others were standing around. No one seemed to know what to do. She froze. Even though she had some long-ago training, she couldn't bring herself to act. The ambulance arrived just moments later, but the man died. The woman felt extremely guilty. After kicking herself around for quite a while, she finally resolved to do something positive. She enrolled in a CPR course taught by the Red Cross and has gone on to become one of their instructors.

Another woman told of assisting at the scene of an automobile accident near her home.

> "I felt the ambulance volunteers (untrained) positioned the man poorly to transport him to the hospital. I questioned them. He died. I felt that perhaps if I had been more assertive — could he have lived?"

There is no way to answer her question. She, like many other women health professionals, hesitated and later was haunted by the question of what might have been.

Besides professional examples, many come from personal lives.

> "When my daughter was having trouble in first grade, I felt she should be retained and suggested this in a conference with both her teacher and principal. She was not retained. Many times since that decision, I have regretted my submissive inaction."

"Submissive inaction" is a very descriptive phrase for what happens to many of us. Decisions affecting you and your family belong in your hands. It is wise to seek expert advice, but the final decision should be yours. Right or wrong, it will be easier to live with your decision than with someone else's.

Finding yourself in a bad job can be just as painful as finding yourself in a bad marriage. It is difficult to admit you have made a poor choice or a poor decision. Instead of resigning yourself to living with your mistake, face up to the situation, take responsibility for the error, and then work on a solution, or a "divorce."

I am not sure if it is loyalty or masochism that binds so many women to joyless, thankless jobs. The health professions have a way of making mincemeat out of bodies, minds, and spirits. Our dying words are, "If I don't do it, who will?" Perhaps if there were no one willing to sacrifice herself in vain, the job situations would be altered, and patient care would improve.

If you find yourself caught in a job that is asking either too much or too little of you, break away. There are bound to be work situations better suited to your needs, talents, abilities, and interests. I just hope they are within the health professions.

We can all help create a climate in which mistakes can be admitted, knowing what colleagues will be quick to help and slow to condemn. Belittling or shaming will only drive mistakes underground, making corrections almost impossible.

The right to give and receive information as a professional

We have come a long way from the days when nurses were not even allowed to disclose a patient's temperature or blood pressure, but we still have a long way to go. Being professional cannot be a sometime thing. Nurses often complain that their "professional" status depends on the time of day. During the day, doctors seem to have little regard for the nurse's opinion. At about suppertime, the nurse suddenly becomes much more knowledgeable and astute in her judgment. After 10 PM, she becomes near genius in her ability to diagnose and treat patients.

Remember that you have the right to approach any other person in the health professions as one professional to another. This can be especially important when telephoning.

> "We recently received a patient from the hospital on the fourth day after a leg amputation. She didn't have a dressing on her stump. Her past history showed frequent postoperative infections. I felt she should have a dressing and called the surgeon's office. I never got beyond the receptionist. Within the next 48 hours, she had two involuntary stools, contaminating her stitches. Three calls later, we still didn't have an order for a dressing, but we put one on anyway. The surgical site became infected, and, would you believe it, it took us a week to get an antibiotic order! The patient had to return to the hospital for treatment of her infected wound. I feel if I had been more assertive and had demanded to talk to the doctor, maybe some of this could have been prevented."

Not being able to get beyond the receptionist can be a real problem. Here is how one woman solved it:

> A social worker was caring for her terminally ill father at home. She found it almost impossible to get through to the doctor on the telephone. His receptionist insisted that she explain the problem to her, and she would pass it along to the doctor. Several messages seemed to have been mislaid or erroneously reported, so the social worker began insisting on speaking to the doctor directly.
>
> She listened patiently to each excuse the receptionist gave but firmly refused to speak to anyone but the doctor. When the receptionist finally ran out of

excuses, the social worker said: "I telephoned the doctor twice yesterday, and he never returned my call. I plan to call every 15 minutes until I am able to speak to the doctor directly." Ten minutes later, the doctor phoned and apologized for the delay and the misunderstandings.

Persistence, perseverance, and a bit of imagination paid off.

What do you do when a co-worker is giving misinformation to patients? Correct them in private if possible. The most important consideration, however, must be the patient's welfare. If the incorrect information is potentially harmful, you have the right and responsibility to intervene on the spot.

"A very confident nonprofessional explained her 'knowledge' of someone's illness. I knew that all her facts weren't correct, but I remained silent."

"I help with the Senior Center Blood Pressure program. I know I should be more firm in advising these people to see a doctor, take their medication, stay on their special diets, and so forth. I feel I'm too wishy-washy with them. I don't want to treat them like children, so I do not like to scold. When I finish, I feel as if I didn't get through to them."

How do you give information without talking down to patients, scolding, or threatening them? The answer is to talk with them as one adult to another. Share what you know in an open, forthright manner. "If you take your medication, this is what you can expect. If you don't take your medication, then this is what you can expect." If the patient refuses to act on the information, that is his right.

Often a little problem solving goes a long way in these situations. You may need to call and make the doctor's appointment right then and there, being sure a ride will be available when the time comes. You may need to find a place to keep a medication in plain view, so they won't forget to take it, or to enlist the help of Meals on Wheels to ensure a proper diet.

The right to act in the best interest of the patient

At no other right will you be hit as frequently as with the old who-do-you-think-you-are dodge. Women in the health professions are too easily intimidated. You have lived a long time, had professional training and perhaps years of professional experience. When it comes time to stand up to a doctor, administrator, or family member, don't be so quick to back down.

You do have the right to act in the best interest of the patient. Here are five situations that illustrate the importance of this right. Consider each. How might you have reacted under the same circumstances?

Situation A

"At 3 AM a patient three months' pregnant called her doctor to report cramping and spotting. He told her to go to work in the morning as usual. At

8 AM the patient came to work. She called me. She was upset, frightened, and felt something was wrong, but she was afraid to 'bother' her doctor, since he didn't seem concerned and was impatient with her. I then spoke to her doctor. He didn't want to be bothered — said it probably wasn't anything and not to take her too seriously.

I was furious about this lack of concern! I felt this patient should be examined and, if it indeed wasn't serious, at least be reassured. So, feeling this way, I consulted the obstetrician who was on call that day and explained her symptoms. He agreed that she needed attention and told me to send her to the hospital immediately where he performed a dilation and curettage at 8:45 AM.

I realize that I could have gotten myself into a lot of trouble, because I went over Doctor 1's head to Doctor 2. However, I believe the patient comes first. In this case, I was successfully assertive."

Situation B

"I work with retarded residents who in recent months have been transferred from crib-type beds to low beds without side rails as part of a normalization program. I spoke to my supervisor about getting side rails for those who have frequent seizures and have been known to fall out of bed, but I received no satisfaction. Finally, after one of the girls fell and sustained a laceration requiring sutures, I spoke with my supervisor again and then communicated with her supervisor. Side rails have now been placed on the bed of that particular resident. I wish I had been more assertive sooner."

Situation C

"I was successfully assertive in a professional situation when it was very unusual for a nurse to question a doctor's order. Following a myocardial infarction, a patient with a very low blood pressure was receiving fluids with aramine added intravenously. The amount of aramine added was so low that we were giving the man too much fluid. I questioned Dr. C about this when he reordered the same strength. He thought and then doubled the amount of aramine. The next time I saw Dr. C, he came up and told me I was very right to question him about his order."

Situation D

"On coming on duty one morning as charge nurse, I immediately checked on a patient who was reported as 'not so good' by the night shift. After checking his vital signs and level of consciousness, I knew that he should be moved to the intensive care unit to receive the constant attention he needed. His personal physician disagreed. When his consulting physician arrived shortly afterward, I again stated my views. The doctor took one look at the patient and ordered him moved to the ICU as fast as possible. The patient remained in the ICU for more than a week."

Situation E

"As a young nurse I was working part-time in the operating room. A woman with severe viral pneumonia receiving continuous oxygen was brought down for a tracheotomy. The floor nurse left her in the hallway, taking the portable oxygen tank with her, after being assured the patient would be in the OR in less than five minutes. Her color was bad, and she had to sit up to breathe. I tried to talk the OR nurses into connecting our oxygen tank, but they didn't want to contaminate it. I brought it out from the storeroom but couldn't find tubing and mask and was told to take it back. The patient finally got into the OR 35 minutes later and died before the tracheotomy could be done."

I am sure this nurse has wished a thousand times that she had gotten oxygen for that woman even if it meant running naked through the halls screaming like a banshee. But it is too late. If you really care about patients, forget your pride. Don't be afraid to question what you see happening to them. Hold your ground until you get results.

The right to be human

A mature woman with two young children was in her third year of medical school. When the children became ill, she found it necessary to drop one of her courses. Even though she was an excellent student both clinically and academically, the assistant dean whom she had to consult quipped: "You will never make a good doctor. Your family is too important to you."

This unkind, inane remark bothered the student so much that she sought professional counseling. The counselor quickly discerned that it was not the student but the dean who needed professional help.

As important and vital as our careers may be, they should not be expected or allowed to obliterate all other facets of our lives. You have the right to sample and enjoy things other than work. To understand patients, it is helpful to have a variety of life experiences.

You are human. Not a saint. Not a martyr. Not a genius. Not a superwoman. Not a super anything. Just a human being.

Sometimes that's difficult to remember when magazines the caliber of *Time* run articles about impending nurses' strikes titled "Rebellion Among Angels" (Aug. 27, 1979). Nurses are not angels. They are all too human.

Many women share times when they were less than perfect in dealing with other people. Even as they recall the events, it is clear that they still harbor guilt resulting from incidents that took place years ago.

"When the doctors sort of said my dad was terminally ill, and Dad felt it, I wish I could have accepted it and talked with him more, instead of trying to mask the truth and be lighthearted."

You cannot be the perfect professional all the time. You can never be professional with members of your own family. You are human. You must grieve and cope and learn. These are your rights, too.

Because you are human, you will get tired, sloppy, impatient, crabby, giddy, greedy, excited, and scared. You will make mistakes. You will not always care deeply about every patient or person in your life. You will not always have power to make the lame walk, the mute talk, or the blind see. Life and death are not under your control. This is not failure. It is just being human.

A public health nurse tells of a patient who simply stopped walking five years ago, although he had no physical impairment. Complications resulting from his inactivity now make it impossible for him to walk. The nurse feels frustrated and guilty because she cannot help this man. She feels responsible for his problems, even though she has only cared for him a short time. It is important to sort out people who want to be salvaged from those who do not. We squander a lot of time and energy trying to save people who do not choose to be saved.

The plight of humans trying to be superhumans may be reflected in this saying posted in an outpatient clinic struggling to keep chronic schizophrenics out of institutions and in the community:

> "We, the willing, led by the unknowing, are doing the impossible for the ungrateful; we have done so much for so long with so little, we are now qualified to do anything with nothing."

The issue of rights can easily become lopsided. Rights need to be tempered with responsibilities. Responsibilities need to be rewarded with rights. We already have a Bill of Rights. What we need is a Bill of Responsibilities.

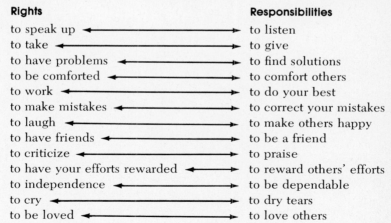

Rights	Responsibilities
to speak up ⟷	to listen
to take ⟷	to give
to have problems ⟷	to find solutions
to be comforted ⟷	to comfort others
to work ⟷	to do your best
to make mistakes ⟷	to correct your mistakes
to laugh ⟷	to make others happy
to have friends ⟷	to be a friend
to criticize ⟷	to praise
to have your efforts rewarded ⟷	to reward others' efforts
to independence ⟷	to be dependable
to cry ⟷	to dry tears
to be loved ⟷	to love others

Take time to add your own ideas for "Rights-Responsibilities." It really is a two-way street. The assertive person knows that abusing either one is destructive to the whole person.

6

Learning to fly

Flying's easy —
it's getting off the ground that's hard.

Flying is easy. It's getting off the ground that's hard.

Begin by reading everything you can get your hands on. Articles on assertiveness training appear in newspapers, magazines, and professional journals. Self-help books are springing up like mushrooms on your bookstore shelves. To help you tell the palatable from the poisonous, an annotated bibliography is provided at the end of this book.

Reading about other people's problems is a fascinating pastime, and you can gather lots of valuable information on the do's and dont's of assertiveness. After you consume a few paperbacks, you will notice how repetitious some of the principles are. The case studies vary, but the formulas for assertive behavior are simple and almost standardized. Examine the problems and situations described for tips on how you can help yourself. Some techniques will appeal to you more than others. After studying assertiveness, do something about it.

That transition between thinking and doing is a difficult one. To help you get off the ground, I strongly recommend participation in an assertiveness training group. Groups are springing up like mushrooms also, and there is bound to be one near you. You can watch the newspaper, or you can be assertive and call the YWCA, your local mental health association, community college, or any psychiatrist or social worker. Tell them you are interested in attending an assertiveness training class or workshop.

Participating in an assertiveness training group will put you in touch with other people who are working on finding the happy medium between being passive and aggressive. It is nice to know you are not alone. A group can give you the support and encouragement you will need to get over your fear of flying.

Often one of the first exercises is to have each member introduce herself to the rest of the group. Immediately, you will see that there are some people who are more bold, confident, and positive than others. Not only do you get a chance to observe others for assertive characteristics, but they get a chance to observe you and give you feedback. The group acts as a mirror to help you see yourself as others see you. They can often pick up clues and cues from your manner and behavior that you would overlook.

Initially, you will work on some fictional exercises, such as having to interrupt someone, sharing differing opinions without being passive or aggressive, exchanging merchandise, or asking for a raise. Later you will work on real-life situations suggested by group members themselves. This gives assertiveness an immediacy and a reality that reading cannot match.

Most of us have experienced moments we would like to relive. Group role play gives you another chance to work through sticky situations. It gives you a chance to say the things you wish you had said, to do the things you wish you had done. This practice prepares you to handle future situations more effectively. The group is also a great place to share "the thrill of victory and the agony of defeat."

Books and groups are important, but they are merely a means to an end. They are not meant to be an end in themselves. Some people have difficulty with this distinction.

Louise is a groupie. She has been a member of one kind of self-help group or another for the past five years. She says she gets nervous if she isn't attending sessions of some kind every week. She shuttles from one group to another in hopes of finding some simple magic that will catapult her out of her colorless life.

During the group session, Louise seems genuinely interested in improving herself. When the group session is over, however, she slips back into her rut, complaining that she just can't seem to get started.

Don't be like Louise. Get started. Recognize that assertiveness training is not magic. It is not a cure-all. It takes work, not wishes, to pull it out of theoretical limbo into everyday living.

Start. Start small.

A colleague thanked me for telling her about a new assertiveness training book I had been reading. She had just finished reading it and exclaimed ecstatically, "After 42 years I finally know how to handle my mother!" Of course, "handling" her mother backfired, and she returned quite sober and dismayed. She was ready to give up assertiveness after one skirmish. Skirmish? It was more like a war.

Let me amend my advice. Start. Start small. Start with strangers.

In relationships as intricate and as intense as mother-daughter, being suddenly assertive can be disastrous. The other person sees an abrupt change as threatening and will probably see your action as aggressive instead of assertive. Becoming assertive in these relationships requires a good deal of thought and planning. Role playing in your group can help you avoid major catastrophes. Before leaping off a cliff and flapping your arms wildly, take time to gain some experience and confidence.

For your first assertive adventure, pick a person with whom you have no emotional investment and whose approval or disapproval should not matter to you. Pick a small situation that has been bothering you, perhaps one involving telephone solicitors, door-to-door salesmen, waitresses, receptionists, or elevator operators.

A good example might be that of the ward clerk at a sprawling state institution who was often sent to the administration building to make copies of certain files. One woman, whose desk was only a few feet from the copying machine, never failed to interrupt her and ask permission to "just run a few copies."

The interruption was so consistent it really began to bother the ward clerk. She felt herself getting more and more angry about it. She brought the situation to the group and received several suggestions. The group role-played some of the alternatives, which ranged from confronting the woman with her behavior to just saying calmly: "Yes, I would mind. I will be done in a few minutes."

The ward clerk decided to confront the woman. The next time the interruption occurred, the clerk said pleasantly: "I know this sounds funny, but you interrupted me Tuesday, Wednesday, and twice yesterday while I was using the copier. I'm beginning to feel a little paranoid."

The woman laughed and apologized. She has not interrupted the clerk again, and they smile and speak when passing.

With assertiveness, nothing succeeds like success. Nothing will give you more courage to be assertive than successfully handling minor daily incidents. Being bold, confident, and positive really pays off. Another asset pays off even more—persistence.

You can get more mileage out of persistence than almost any other assertive technique. On the surface it seems simple enough, but getting women in the health professions to be persistent is incredibly difficult. We bend over backward to see the other person's point of view. We hate to offend anyone. We pride ourselves on being fair, flexible, and open-minded. Someone quipped that we try to be so open-minded our brains fall out.

Getting women to speak up is easier than getting them to stand behind what they say. At the first sign of conflict (an icy stare, a questioning look, a put-down, a refusal), women beat a hasty retreat. Before you retreat, repeat what you said. Once is not enough. Twice may not be enough. Repeat your case over and over again in a calm, even voice. Do not become angry or argumentative.

> "I discovered that a co-worker with approximately the same status but fewer years of service and experience earns 88 cents an hour more than I do. I approached the personnel director. I thought I was assertive as I stated my case and asked for job comparison, capabilities, productivity, etc. I was promised something would be done. Nothing came of this. I've also done nothing more."

This example illustrates the importance of setting time limits. Granted, the personnel director might not be able to correct the situation on the spot, but he or she needs to know you expect action—soon! As you are concluding your session say, "I will check back with you Thursday morning."

On Thursday morning if there is no resolution say, "I will check back with you Tuesday afternoon." This confident approach will make it impossible for the administrator to conveniently forget your plight.

Persist. Persist cheerfully. The director will soon tire of your appearances and resolve the issue.

In many instances it pays to be a woman of few words. State what you want or what is bothering you in as few words as possible. The fewer words you use, the more difficult it is to argue with you. If you remain steadfast and single-minded, you will not be lured off onto tangents or sidetracked by smooth talkers who wish to cloud the issue.

"Our unit needs another nurse."

"Do you know what would happen if every unit in the hospital requested one more nurse?"

"No, I do not. I just know that our unit needs another nurse to give safe patient care."

Once you decide on the course of action that is in the best interest of the patient, stand up for your decision. If you persevere, you may be surprised at how quickly others will retreat or at least withdraw to reconsider the situation. Being flexible is fine, but many situations in life require backbone.

"While working in a small hospital in eastern Oregon, I received a phone call at home from the Director of Nurses asking me to accompany a patient with a severed spinal cord and a tracheostomy on an ambulance trip to the university medical center about a hundred miles away. I had been his floor nurse on the 11 PM to 7 AM shift the past few days, and the patient had indicated he had a lot of confidence in my nursing care. His construction company would pay $100 to the nurse who went on the ambulance trip. Another nurse had indicated that she wanted to go in my place.

I had worked all night, and the phone had awakened me. My initial reaction was that I felt too tired and sleepy to go on the trip, which was to start right then. After I hung up the phone and felt more awake, I knew I wanted to go and called the director back. She said I would have to call the nurse who was taking my place. This nurse insisted on going herself, because, she said, she needed the money. I gave in and let her go in my place. I later found out she was not very interested in what kind of patient care she gave.

I felt I had let the patient down by not going after he had requested me to be the one to go. The patient was very apprehensive about his tracheostomy and depressed because he was a paraplegic from a construction job injury he had just received. I have always regretted my not being more assertive with her."

In this situation, the second nurse outpersisted the first nurse. The money and the fact that the first nurse had momentarily refused to make the trip are side issues. The crux of the matter, and the point that cannot be argued, is the fact that the patient requested her to go with him.

To handle this in a more assertive manner, she should listen politely to every excuse or argument the second nurse gives and then calmly and stead-fastly repeat: "But the patient requested me, and I intend to go with him."

When the second nurse says she needs the money, the first nurse should reply, "I am sorry you are disappointed, but the patient requested me, and I intend to go with him." When she reminds her that she initially turned down his request, she should say: "That is true. But the patient requested me, and I intend to go with him."

After three or four exchanges, the second nurse will see that the first nurse has no intention of backing down and will drop the matter. She may be angry and disappointed, but the patient will be appreciative and relieved. When it comes to offending someone to defend the patient, there really is no choice. If you let the patient and yourself down, you will be haunted by another I-wish-I-had-it-to-do-all-over-again situation.

Here is an excellent example of assertive persistence in action:

"Last summer I visited my son and his wife and joined them at their church picnic. Lots of people and happy children.

I noticed one child who was continually scratching. His mother told him not to scratch: 'It'll only make it worse!' I went over and looked. I even asked him to raise his T-shirt. His body was covered with large hives. I told the mother the child should be taken to a doctor. She replied, 'Oh, he probably got into some nettles. They'll go away.'

But I didn't like the look on the child's face — it was apprehensive. I followed the child's movements for about five minutes and saw his frantic efforts to scratch and yet try to resist that urge. The hives got bigger and spread over his arms and onto his face.

I approached the mother again. She really wasn't that alarmed and said she would apply cold compresses. I told her I was a nurse and I really thought the child needed medical attention. She informed me she would go ahead with the cold compresses. I cornered the minister and told him the child might be in danger and why. He was more persuasive with the mother than I, and she did take her son to the hospital emergency room.

A week later I got a very nice note thanking me for urging medical attention for the child. She informed me that they almost lost him because of the severity of the reaction."

This woman had enough guts to speak up and to keep speaking up until she got results. After the initial rebuff by the mother, she didn't just shrug her shoulders and say, "Oh, well, I tried, didn't I?"

Follow this woman's example. Don't make a half-hearted attempt to be assertive and then be disappointed when it doesn't quite work. Throw body, soul, and ego into what you are doing. If you sit in a corner and wait until you get enough confidence to be assertive, you will be covered with cobwebs. Confidence comes *after* you dare to assert yourself. The more you assert yourself, the more confident you will become. The more confident you become, the easier it is to be assertive.

When learning to be assertive, the use of "I" is imperative. How else can you articulate true feelings, needs, and expectations in an unmistakable manner?

I feel . . .
I expect . . .
I want . . .
I choose . . .
I decide . . .
I plan . . .
I believe . . .
I am (angry, confused, delighted, disappointed) . . .

"I-messages" tend to be less threatening and more effective in keeping communication open than "you-messages." For example, consider the difference between each of the following pairs:

> "I get so angry when promises are broken!"
> "You make me so mad! You never keep a promise!"

> "I appreciate your opinion, but I believe this is best for me."
> "You ought to mind your own business."

> "I expect you to pick up your dirty clothes."
> "You are such a slob! Look at this mess."

Pretend you have received an unfair grade and have decided to talk with your instructor about it. As you enter his office, which words would invite explanation without threatening or blaming?

> "You made a mistake in my grade."
> "Why did I get a C?"
> "I don't understand my grade."

The first response is an accusation that automatically prompts the instructor to defend his position or deny the problem exists even before he investigates it. The second response is also less than optimum because "whys" are always threatening and usually irrelevant. In this case, the third response would be best.

The following situation revolves around just such an unfair grade:

> After years as a homemaker, Martha returned to college. She thrived on hard work and was making excellent grades. In her anthropology class, however, she was aware of a "personality clash" with the young, male instructor. For some reason he simply didn't like her no matter how hard she tried to please him.

On all of her exams, projects, and written assignments she had received A's and B's. You can imagine her surprise and disappointment when she received a C for the course.

Unfortunately, Martha did nothing about her grade. Six years later the incident was still bothering her enough that she asked her assertiveness training group to help work out step-by-step actions that could have helped her prevent this nagging conflict.

The group devised the following six steps as the best course of action for anyone caught in a similar situation:

1. Don't take the grade personally (at least initially). Assume the best, not the worst.
2. Gather documentation: tests, projects, papers.
3. Make an appointment. Approach him with "I am puzzled about my grade." Make no lengthy arguments or explanations.
4. Wait calmly. Give him time to check his grade book. Remember, it may be an honest mistake. Even if he did it maliciously, he has a face-saving way out by blaming the error on a secretary or a computer. The "why" is not important. Your only concern is acquiring the correct grade.
5. After presenting your documentation, if he still refuses to alter the grade and you are unsatisfied with his reasoning, say, "I disagree with your assessment of my performance. I will speak to the division chairman."
6. Follow through. Stay centered on the task and avoid any temptation to lapse into personality conflict.

It may take five minutes to remedy the situation. It may take five weeks. Any effort is a small price to pay to avoid six years of brooding.

Exploring all the "should haves" is useful if what you learn can be applied to new situations. It is not useful to torment yourself with "I wish I would have said . . . ," "I *should* have . . . ," or "Why didn't I . . . ?"

Once the grade becomes ancient history, as it has for Martha, there is only one thing left to do: GET OVER IT. That's another motto suitable for framing.

The courage or timidity with which you handle strangers is some indication of how difficult it will be to assert yourself with the important people in your life. Before you move assertiveness into close relationships, imagine the most awful thing that could happen. The extremes usually involve getting a divorce or getting fired. Conjuring up dire consequences this way makes most women realize how unrealistic and exaggerated their fears are. They discover they have been passive to protect their pride and to keep their "nice woman" and "good mother" images from being tarnished.

Once you decide to be assertive with your family and friends, start slowly and start small. Your new behavior is bound to be questioned or attacked. If you are unsure of yourself, you may suffer a setback. Even if you make a crash landing the first time or two, don't give up.

Naturally, there is some risk in altering your behavior. Change is always threatening, but it can also be invigorating. Here is a beautiful example of assertiveness within close personal relationships.

> "My sister-in-law, 45 years old, who is mentally handicapped, has been living with us six months out of a year since her mother died three years ago. She promptly began changing our daily lives (we have five children) with temper tantrums, demands, and general uncooperativeness (wouldn't allow me to wash her hair or clothes, wet the bed on purpose, and so forth).
>
> She stated, 'You're not my sister, and I don't have to listen to you.' I was admonished by her brother and sister to be glad my children were normal and to accept Mandy as she was.
>
> After eight weeks of great tension, I decided that this unhappy situation must change for my own sanity and the happiness of our children, who saw all of Mandy's whims being met while they were required to adhere to good manners, sharing, and working together.
>
> I asserted myself by explaining to Mandy and the relatives that this was our home too and we were entitled to enjoy it, and that meant Mandy must adjust. We praised her for any good she did and took away privileges, such as her daily bottle of pop (before, she freely demanded up to five bottles a day at one point) or TV watching or dessert, for misdemeanors. I insisted she participate in our area center for the handicapped against much family anger.
>
> Mandy has adjusted quite well, and the daily problems we do have I feel I can cope with because I am in control again. Life here is much better now since I asserted myself after realizing 'This is my home.' Mandy has lived up to our increased expectations of her in many ways, and we are back to loving each other."

A lot of perseverance went into turning this destructive situation around. It has the happy ending that many women report when they finally break out of the passive-aggressive-guilt cycle: "We are back to loving each other."

7

How to tell
a turkey
to stuff it

You don't have to be nuts to work here.

What's the most difficult word in the English language to pronounce? For many, it's "no."

Recently, whole books have been devoted to teaching men and women how to say no. That seemingly simple goal has also been the focus of countless assertiveness training groups.

A popular criticism of assertiveness training is that it just gives an excuse to people who are already bullies to go ahead and take advantage of other people. On the contrary, the goal of assertiveness training is not to help you take advantage of other people, but to stop other people from taking advantage of you. And the quickest way to stop people from taking advantage of you is to say no.

The necessarily negative flavor of all this has turned off some women. They sense a rather belligerent and uncaring aura around assertiveness. It is true that many women, while learning to be assertive, go through a negative phase much like the one toddlers experience. That little word "no" has incredible force. Even when you were only two feet tall, you could bring things to a grinding halt by saying no. For the adult woman, it is like recapturing some long-forgotten power.

Like using an atrophied muscle, the more you exercise your prerogative to say no, the easier it becomes. First you find you can refuse requests on the telephone and later face to face. You begin by saying no to strangers and progress to friends and family. Ultimately, you are able to hold your own with assorted authorities, such as bosses, teachers, doctors, and even the clergy. Hallelujah!

But the purpose of assertiveness training is not to turn you into a no-it-all. Anyone who doesn't progress beyond the negative phase has a case of arrested development. The beauty of assertiveness is that it frees you to say "yes." Yes to all the people, places, and things you really want to get involved with.

It takes some time and effort to understand assertiveness. Throughout the years, we have been conditioned to label behavior as either passive or aggressive. We are now realizing that sandwiched between those two extremes is a third area: assertive behavior.

There is a lot of talk about the fine line between being assertive and being aggressive. Women are petrified that they will cross this line without even knowing it. Whereas it may be uncomfortable to be passive, it is abominable to be aggressive. If this is worrying you, take heart. The line between assertiveness and aggressiveness is not as fine or as fragile as you may think.

Consult any dictionary and you will find some interesting words and phrases used to define *assertive* and *aggressive*. *Assertive* is defined with words like "bold," "confident," and "positive." *Aggressive* is defined with words like "hostile," "injurious," "violating," and "destructive." It is difficult to believe there is much danger of confusing the two. The dictionary does list *aggressive* as a synonym for *assertive*, but that is merely cause for semantic stumbling, not for stumbling in real life.

> "I was waiting for morning report when the night nurse came in to tell the group something that was not on the taped report. Everyone, including me, was busy chatting. She spoke my name loudly and said, 'Shut up! I'm trying to tell you something!'
>
> I immediately shut up, and so did everyone else. She was very assertive, but I was not. I did not know what to say."

The night nurse in this situation was not assertive. She was aggressive. By the time you finish this chapter, you will have a good idea of what to say to a person who humiliates you like this in front of others.

In today's jargon, passive behavior has been labeled "nonassertive," that is, behavior that is not bold, not confident, and not positive. I prefer to use "passive" instead of "nonassertive." The dictionary defines *passive* as lethargic, inert, submissive, exhibiting no gain or control, and receiving or enduring without resistance. That seems much more descriptive and accurate when talking about women in the health professions. We have been lethargic, inert, and submissive. We have no control over the health care system, and we have endured much abuse and misuse without resistance.

No dictionary will give you the following definition for "turkey," but for the purpose of this book, a *turkey* will be defined as anyone who wants to take advantage of you: anyone who wants to gobble up your time, energy, talent, money, patience, good will, humor, or self-respect. Rediscovering the word "no" is an excellent beginning in learning to deal with the turkeys in your life.

For example, the telephone rings, and you are asked to collect for the Annual Athlete's Foot Fund. Assuming that no one close to you is suffering from terminal athlete's foot and that you really have no interest in their annual drive, how will you respond? You have three basic options: passive, aggressive, and assertive.

The passive response (lethargic, inert, submissive) is to listen to the entire spiel, offer weak excuses (each of which is expertly dismissed by the solicitor), and finally give in and agree to march for athlete's foot, kicking yourself every step of the way.

The aggressive response (hostile, injurious, destructive) might be to curse, belittle the cause, slam the receiver down abruptly, or rip the phone off the wall.

The assertive response is to say "No" or "No, thank you." Offer no excuses, but boldly, confidently, and positively decline. Being assertive, you will already have offered your time, talent, and financial backing to organizations that really do interest you. This type of positive action on your part will go a long way in easing any guilt feelings you may have about not being able to save the whole world.

There is certainly nothing wrong in agreeing to collect for a charity, *unless* you feel angry with yourself for doing so. After hanging up the phone, many women are furious with themselves for not being able to refuse anyone anything.

The passive woman usually finds her life cluttered with odds and ends that no one else wants to do. She has never learned to value herself, much less her time. Although she doesn't actively seek additional chores, she has never learned how to refuse effectively. Her silence is taken as consent.

She believes in giving until it hurts. Even when it hurts, she continues to give until the pain is excruciating. Then comes the straw that breaks her back. Some minor request or inconvenience suddenly sets her off like a skyrocket. There is an emotional holocaust, with shaming, blaming, screaming, and crying. Afterward, she usually feels intense guilt. Ashamed and remorseful, she quietly slips back into the passive routine. Her life might be diagrammed like this:

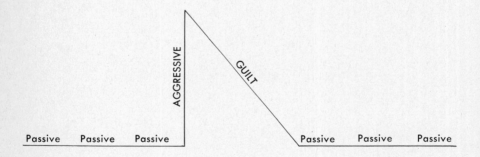

To interrupt this self-defeating cycle, it is necessary to convert many of the passive encounters into assertive ones. That way there is no mountainous buildup of minor incidents, and an emotional avalanche is prevented.

If after any exchange you feel used, guilty, angry, stupid, hurt, violated, or destroyed, then you have been the victim of aggression. If after any exchange the other person experiences these feelings, then you have been the aggressor.

It is vital to remember that a manipulator needs a manipulatee. When you start refusing to be manipulated, the other person is bound to be somewhat disappointed, irritated, or inconvenienced, but that is a far cry from being violated or destroyed.

Do not make the mistake of letting every turkey trot all over you until you lose control and try to make hash out of all of them at once. The secret of success is to tackle one turkey at a time. Try this for your meditation chant: "One turkey at a time . . . one turkey at a time . . . one turkey at a time."

Here are some examples given by women in the health professions. Their situations may sound all too familiar to you.

Turkey 1

Getting stuck with lots of personally meaningless activities is the most common complaint of women who fail to be assertive.

> "I just let someone assign me to another committee in an organization, when I'm already doing my share. I should have been assertive and said, 'No, thank you, but I can't help out on that committee at this time.' Instead I'm doing the extra job, but I'm not happy with myself about it! It's no one's fault but my own! My lack of assertiveness springs from a lack of self-confidence."

This woman had an excellent assertive response but did not use it. Or, if she did use it, she was not convincing. Refusing effectively takes practice. Be firm. If you waver, you will probably end up with the extra assignment.

Resist the urge to make excuses for refusing. It is difficult to invent convincing excuses on the spot, and most women feel guilty if they lie. However, the penalty for telling the truth—that there is no compelling reason for you to refuse the task—is to be given the chore.

Stick with the concrete theme: "No . . . not at this time." Repeat it as often as necessary.

Turkey 2

> "The reason I am calling you is that I am handicapped. . . ."

This preamble is a telephone solicitor's way of trying to sell you everything from rug cleaners to candles, greeting cards to light bulbs. The word "handicapped" is meant to trigger feelings of sympathy and guilt. Whenever the flags of sympathy and guilt begin flying, beware! You are about to be manipulated.

After a brief introductory appeal, there is usually a pause in which they ask if they may now read through a list of products to see if you would be interested in any of them. This is where I say, "No, thank you, I am not interested in purchasing anything today, but thank you for calling. Goodbye." I learned to do this the hard way. I have a cupboard full of household products that cost twice as much as name-brand items and work half as well.

Saying no to random hits for money is often difficult. After all, how can you refuse someone less fortunate than yourself? Politely. You refuse politely.

Women in the health professions have deep-rooted needs to help others. If you do not want to become bitter and burned out, it is essential to designate who these others are. You are only human. Your resources are limited. The assertive response is to seek out individuals and organizations with which you want to share your resources.

Turkey 3

"Our pastor said I should tell my daughter that he 'wouldn't love her any-more if she didn't join the junior choir.' Luckily, I came up with the statement that 'I couldn't do that because it sounds too unchristian.' His request still bothers me, and I have great difficulty going to his service. I've seen him being manipulative at church meetings."

Whether the person is a minister, scientist, administrator, or professor, each is human. Each has a NOT OK. Some handle the NOT OK in a healthy manner, and some do not.

We want to be perfect. We want others to be perfect too—especially those in positions of authority. When they fail to be perfect, we may be sad or furious. At first we may deny their imperfection and continue to follow faithfully. Even when the evidence is overwhelming, it is difficult to denounce a person whose position you have been taught to respect or revere.

Trust your feelings, intuition, and experience. Do not put your trust in degrees, rank, or position. A turkey is a turkey, even if he wears a clerical collar.

Turkey 4

"I worked with one nurse's aide who never seemed to be able to get her work done. She was always making excuses and getting somebody to help her, no matter how light her workload was for the day.

I always tried to cover for her, because she said she needed the job so badly. So I would give her easy patients. But one day she even had me helping her with bed-making! I was so mad at myself, I blew up and told her I just couldn't cope with her excuses."

Many marginal people seem to be attracted to less-skilled jobs in the health professions. Blinded by huge needs of their own, they find it nearly impossible to deal with patient needs. Women in the health professions are more tolerant of these employees than private industry would be.

There is a lot of Mother Hen in all of us. We try to have a "therapeutic" relationship with everyone. Our rescue needs spill over from patients onto co-workers, family, neighbors, and strangers. We are good listeners, patient, forgiving, and long-suffering. We are suckers for a hard-luck story.

Time after time, inadequate employees add to our burden, infuriate fellow workers, and lower the quality of patient care, but we feel a responsibility to carry them, to cover for them. We give and give and give, while they take and take and take. When we are mentally, emotionally, and physically exhausted, we explode. There is an angry tirade, and afterward we feel guilty. We want to minimize their shortcomings, make excuses for their behavior, and give them another chance, thus perpetuating a miserable situation.

When an employee fails to do her fair share of work, it is important to intervene long before the situation becomes critical. Begin collecting data when the problem is first noticed. Keep a record of the number of tasks she did and did not finish, the number and content of excuses given, the times late for work, times absent, and errors made. Then sit down with the employee privately, and describe the situation in detail.

In working with psychiatric patients, it is often said that you will get the behavior you expect. If you expect them to be bizarre and violent, they will not disappoint you. Similarly, if you expect your employee to be late, slow, inefficient, and helpless, that is certainly the behavior you will get.

Take a bold, confident, positive approach: "This is what I expect. Let's try it out for a week and see how it goes." Help her set goals and do some problem solving, but resist the temptation to adopt her or her problems as your own.

After a week or two, sit down and reevaluate what you see happening. Praise her for achievements. However, if the problem persists, tell her frankly that she is simply not working out and that you intend to recommend she be dismissed.

There may be crying, pleading, or swearing, but through it all you must keep your eye on the patient's best interest. You are responsible for the patient's comfort and safety. Do not confuse the work relationship with a therapeutic relationship.

Turkey 5

"I was late for a class as a student nurse because I had duties to finish in the recovery room. The instructor was most unkind in her remarks and embarrassed me in front of my classmates.

I would have liked to tell her my thoughts and reasons for being tardy but felt insecure and somewhat inferior — since she was the teacher."

Once again we have the problem of inferior people in superior positions. Insecure instructors need to keep students ever mindful of their subordinate role. This instructor was rude. At the very least, she deserves a BM sticker.

Whenever you are treated unjustly, do not suffer silently. Face the instructor after class and say: "I felt very embarrassed and angry when you made those remarks about my being late. I would like to give you the reasons for my behavior now if you would be willing to listen."

If you are afraid of repercussions from openly sharing your feelings with the instructor, let off steam in a less direct way—smack a tennis ball, jog, write a letter detailing your feelings and then destroy it, or share your humiliation with a good friend who will listen. Whatever you do, do not swallow your feelings. They will make you sick.

Please savor and remember the humiliations you endure as a student or a subordinate. When you arrive at the superior position, do not do unto others as you have been done unto.

Turkey 6

"A patient was emotionally ill and was hospitalized in a general hospital. She had physical symptoms caused by her emotional illness. Every time her husband came, she became upset, short of breath, and extremely nervous. Then her husband would hassle us about getting the doctor to come and see her immediately. When the doctor was contacted, he would chuckle, make off-hand remarks about her nerves, and let us handle the upset husband.

If I had it to do over again, I would have referred the doctor to the psychiatrist! I would have also pointed out to the husband what effect he was having on his wife. Maybe it wouldn't have helped anyone, but I would have felt better about the whole situation."

The doctor's mobility is indeed enviable. He can leave for surgery, his office, another unit, or the golf course, but the nurse is confined to the immediate situation. She is left holding the bag literally and figuratively.

Again, your actions should be guided by the best interest of the patient. Obviously, she is not being helped. Document on the chart what you see happening, including the telephone calls to the doctor and his responses. Telephone the doctor, and, when you get him on the line, hand the phone to the husband. Try to make sure the husband's visit coincides with the doctor's rounds at least once.

This is one of the many times when it is handy to have a psychiatrist willing to consult with your staff. If a psychiatrist is not available to you, get organized and petition the administration for this sort of consulting service. Pester them until you get it.

If this were my situation, I would probably speak to the wife alone about my observations. For example:

"I've noticed something kind of interesting, and I was wondering if you had noticed it, too. During the day, you seem relaxed and at ease. But after supper, when your husband arrives, you get short of breath and seem very nervous. Is that the way it seems to you, too?"

She may be relieved to have the obvious put into words, and a torrent of hopes and fears may tumble out. She may be furious and leave the hospital in a huff. Either way, hearing those words from a professional source may make her more accepting of future psychiatric treatment.

Turkey 7

Whoever said "Sticks and stones may break my bones, but words can never hurt me" was wrong. I have not seen any women in the health professions battered physically, but I have seen many who were scared and scarred by words. Being sensitive to others is one of our strengths, but it also leaves us very vulnerable to verbal abuse.

"While I was working the 3 to 11:30 shift one evening, a doctor began shouting at me for something that happened during the day shift. The fact that I hadn't been in the hospital at the time of the incident didn't seem to matter to him. There are many things I wish I had had the nerve to tell him."

Women tend to personalize verbal attacks. Even though this nurse knows she is not responsible for the incident, she feels some guilt by association. The error was made on this unit; this is my unit; therefore, I am guilty. This is the logical illogic that makes many women shoulder shame and blame for events beyond their control.

The passive response is to feel sad or depressed or to smolder silently. The aggressive response is to shout back at the doctor and usually to feel angry with yourself afterward for losing control. The assertive response is to speak up. After the doctor finishes shouting, tell him calmly: "I can see you are upset (concerned, furious, whatever), but I was not present at the time of the event. However, I would be willing to work with you to make matters right."

Learning to speak up to authorities is a major hurdle for women in the health professions. One nurse was working on a neonatal unit when three babies in critical condition were transferred in at the same time. Staffing was poor, and she had only a licensed practical nurse to help her. The doctor was very nervous and demanding. At one point, she simply turned to him and said, "I only have two hands; just tell me what you want done first." He smiled and was much more understanding then.

Another crusty old physician had the irritating habit of talking down to the nursing staff. He kept making snide remarks, as though he thought the staff was planning to destroy all the good he intended to do. Finally, one nurse spoke up: "Look, Dr. K, I care just as much about Mrs. C as you do—perhaps even more. I intend to do everything in my power to help her get well." After that confrontation, he mellowed considerably and continued to seek out that particular nurse to work with whenever possible.

Turkey 8

"Six RN's, six student nurses, four LPN's, and three aides left at 3:30, leaving me with one LPN and two aides to care for 23 patients, four of whom could be listed in poor condition (the rest were children under age 11). At the stroke of 4 one of the not-poor patients began hemorrhaging and was clinically in shock. His doctor was not in the house, nor could I get through to his clinic (busy line). I was calling from the room phone. On my way out of the room to get more dressings and Ace bandages, I told the LPN to call the emergency room doctor. Just at that moment, the head nurse came off the elevator from a meeting. The emergency room doctor and the attending doctor came within moments, and the boy was rushed to the operating room for resuturing of severed leg arteries. (The emergency room doctor had obtained x-rays and had started an IV before the attending doctor got there.)

After the boy was in the operating room, my head nurse told me I must never call 'just any doctor while the attending doctor is in his office,' nor should I 'ever let an LPN call a doctor when the symptoms require an RN to interpret them,' and this was not a 'Blue Code' situation, so calling the emergency room doctor from his department was wasteful of his time.

I am afraid I totally lost my temper and quite literally yelled at her, 'I wish it had been an arrest—I know CPR!—but if he bleeds to death I have nothing!' And I stammered and stuttered about this being an example of her poor staffing techniques . . . and I'm only one person. . . . It makes me mad all over again!"

Women frequently complain about supervisors and head nurses with Victorian attitudes and antiquated rule books. Years ago, nurses got the starch out of their uniforms, but some can't seem to get it out of their minds. You know the type: the head nurse who would interrupt mouth-to-mouth resuscitation to have you pick up the linen off the floor.

Many nurses report working in situations with criminal understaffing. We have become accustomed to making do. We keep plugging holes in the dike, never facing the fact that a flood is inevitable. We always hesitate a little too long, until an emergency or disaster forces action. Allowing 1.67 nurses for 30 patients may look fine on budget sheets, but, when translated into people instead of percentages, it may fall short.

In this situation, the staff nurse did act in the best interest of her patient. The fact that recalling the incident makes her mad all over again means that there has never been proper resolution. The emotional explosion on the scene did not clear the air. Instead of fuming and festering in silence, the nurse should speak up again. This time, it would be better to choose a more neutral occasion and place. Approach the head nurse privately:

> "When that boy began bleeding and I could not reach his doctor, I was tense and frightened. He was in shock. I knew I had to work fast. I felt hurt and angry that you chose those moments to scold me. I think we have some serious staffing problems here, and I would like to help work out a more satisfactory arrangement."

The head nurse's criticism was ill timed. When emotions are running high, resist the urge to criticize. At times like this, the staff needs support. Stand up for them. Stand behind them. A comment that tells the staff nurse you realize what she had just gone through will go a long way in defusing emotions. For example: "You must have been awfully concerned about the boy. It is so frustrating not to be able to reach the right doctor during an emergency."

If there is reason to be upset about the way an emergency situation is handled, wait for a more neutral time to correct any errors in procedure. Get the staff together and review policies. Help them do some problem solving, so that next time difficulties arise, things will go more smoothly.

It's time to try your own hand at telling a turkey to stuff it. Read the following situation. Try to imagine yourself standing at the doorway. Picture your own hospital administrator and his office.

Broken appointment

You stand at the door of the hospital administrator's office and knock lightly: "Excuse me, but I believe I have a 3 o'clock appointment with you."

The administrator glances up from his desk and says, "I'm too busy to see you today." He looks down at his desk and begins shuffling papers.

How would you respond?

1. Physical response (specifically what happens to your body in such situations—perspire, sigh, palpitations, weak knees, etc.): _____

_____

2. Emotional response (fear, anger, frustration, humiliation, etc.):

_____

3. Verbal response:
   a. What I would like to say to him is, "_____
   _____."
   b. But, a more effective thing to say would be, "_____
   _____."

Setting up situations in this format has proved helpful in working with both large and small groups. A written exercise gives each person an opportunity to actively describe her feelings, have the fun of "telling the turkey off," and then settle down to the most important task: articulating a response that will keep communication open without compromising her position.

After everyone has had time to complete the exercise, ask for volunteers to call out "one word that describes something that happens to you physically" and then "one emotion you would experience as you stood at the door." What a relief to discover you are not alone! Others clench, tremble, blush, cry. Others feel sad, put down, outraged, humiliated.

Most will be delighted to share their snappy comebacks under "What I would like to say is '_____.'" The responses are hilarious, and laughter is a great tension releaser.

After the giggles subside, the group settles down to the difficult task of forming words and selecting actions that communicate effectively. Be prepared for Freudian slips and lapses into passive or aggressive behavior. Although there is never one "right" answer, it will be obvious to the group that some choices are better than others. They will quickly chime in with variations, suggestions, or modifications. Help them look for responses that are confident, positive, brief, task centered, and nonthreatening enough to invite further communication. Help them focus on I-messages instead of you-messages.

None of the situations in this book is fabricated. All have come from workshop participants. Please feel free to use any of them when working in a classroom or workshop setting. You will soon discover, however, that each group is teeming with examples of its own. You would be wise to take a few moments and let the participants write a description of a situation (personal or professional) in which they were assertive or *wish* they had been more assertive.

To help ensure anonymity, give them scratch paper and tell them not to sign their names. If the situation described is a sensitive one that would embarrass the writer or another group member, have these persons put a large star at the top of the page to indicate that it should not be shared. On the other hand, if they have a situation they would love to have analyzed or role-played, have them print "PLEASE USE" in large letters at the top of the page. Using situations that come directly from the group enables everyone to become more personally involved and gives the group a greater sense of accomplishment when they reach a solution.

•   •   •

Daily encounters with turkeys cannot be avoided. Your best defense is to value yourself, your time, and your resources. When you learn to do that, saying no will be less painful and saying yes will be a pleasure. When turkeys get the best of you and you blow up, do not brood or punish yourself. Just take the experience as a reminder to tackle one turkey at a time. Most important, do not swallow your feelings and opinions. Learn to speak up. "Let's talk, turkey."

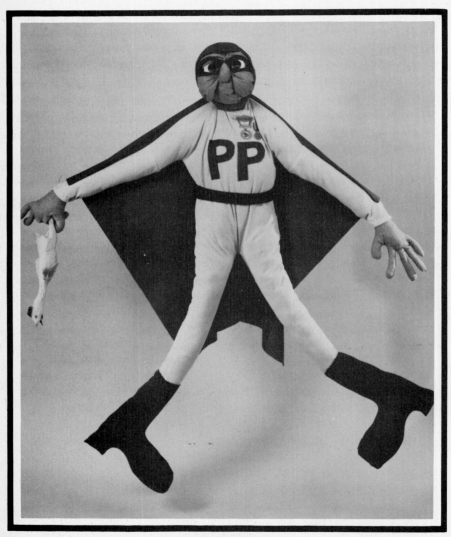

Patient Protector.

Look—up in the air! It's a bird! It's a plane! No—it's PATIENT PRO-TECTOR!

Patient Protector—idol of the infirm, champion of the weak, defender of dignity.

Who would believe that in real life Patient Protector is just a mild-mannered health care worker? But at the first sign of patient distress, this quick-change artist emerges from the linen closet as Patient Protector!

Stunningly attired in a jaundice-yellow jumpsuit, blood-red cape, bile-green belt and mask, and cyanotic-blue boots, Patient Protector perches atop the patient's bed, scrutinizing all who enter the room. Armed only with a rubber chicken and a little legal Latin, Patient Protector defends patients from the high and the mighty as well as the low and the loathsome.

Patient Protector—able to translate medical mumbo jumbo faster than the speed of sound, able to leap across to the corner drugstore for cheap aspirin and Kleenex, able to fetch a burger and fries when the hospital sends up creamed liver and banana casserole.

Who dares tackle tiresome visitors and tacky technicians? Who dares stump students who have neglected to do their homework? Who forces dietitians to down their own concoctions? Who heckles head nurses, interrogates interns, and razzes residents? Who waddles down the hall behind pompous physicians quacking all the way? Who? Patient Protector!

Although most would agree that Patient Protector would be nothing without such an outlandish uniform, we are reluctant to accept the cliché that "clothes make the man." We have an aversion to thinking that something as superficial as clothing can have such impact. It makes people seem so shallow. After all, image is only a reflection. Image has no substance. It's what's inside that counts. But advertisers will tell you "it's what's up front that counts"; according to motivational researcher John T. Molloy, image is all that counts.

Molloy is billed as an "image engineer," and he has research results to show that how you decorate yourself and your surroundings can spell the difference between success and failure. In his initial study, he found that students worked harder and more conscientiously for teachers who dressed formally than for teachers who did not. Taking these findings, he quit teaching and launched a highly profitable career as writer, researcher, and consultant to individuals and companies seeking success.

A fascinating article based on his work appeared in *Medical Dimensions,* December 1975, titled "How Your Personal Image Can Help Your Career." Doctors who follow his advice about wardrobes and waiting rooms are supposed to attract patients who pay bills promptly and don't bother them outside of office hours. Molloy recommends a very restricted range of suits, shirts, ties, and shoes to be worn, adding such fine details as *always* having a leather band on your expensive but unostentatious watch.

There are two particularly striking things about the article. First, there are only four brief paragraphs counseling women physicians on their image. Second, the picture chosen to represent the woman is reminiscent of a 1930s *male* movie star. The model wears a highly tailored, thick tweed suit, complete with shirt and tie. The visual message: Dress like a man.

Perhaps the paucity of material available for women is what inspired Molloy to write a new book: *The Woman's Dress for Success Book.** Also along this line is Michael Korda's *Success!*† Both tell women how to dress for success and power. (Ever wonder why so many books for women are written by men?)

In very condensed form, the rules say powerful, successful women will shun anything feminine or fashionable. They will be clothed in very tailored, dark-colored suits, shod with dark-colored leather pumps, and capped with maroon fedoras with a little feather. Double knits look cheap, so they are a no-no. Since handbags frighten men, successful women will carry only expensive leather briefcases, and they will sign everything with gold pens.

Where does all of this leave you and me? Hundreds of thousands of us are wearing white double knits with orthopedic shoes, sporting Timexes on Twist-o-Flexes, carrying enema cans instead of briefcases, and flicking our Bics. Nothing about us communicates success or power. In fact, our attire hardly distinguishes us from any waitress in an all-night beanery.

One nurse from the East Coast reported shopping in a major department store whose uniform section was marked "NURSES AND OTHER DOMESTICS." Molloy says, "If you dress like a vice president, you will be treated like a vice president." It would logically follow that, if you dress like a domestic, you will be treated like a domestic. When discussing image and the woman health professional, one nurse summed it up this way: "Most of the time, I feel I am invisible."

Being invisible does have its advantages. It is safer to blend into the background. You will most likely be left alone. Many women are content to just float along as another forgettable face amid an endless sea of white. They are content, until they want to call attention to a problem or make changes in patient care policy.

That's when being invisible puts you at a terrible disadvantage. You are so easy to ignore. You are totally forgettable. People with power to make changes may appear to listen but not take you seriously enough to act on your

---

*Chicago, 1977, Follett Publishing Co.
†New York, 1977, Random House, Inc.

suggestions. You have no muscle. There are no threats you can enforce. They know if they stall temporarily, you will just drift away into the background. The system remains unchanged.

It would be nice if powerful people cared more about issues than images, but it may be naive to think they do. The powerful are very image-oriented. Their main concern is making sure everything looks good—especially on paper. Why else would medical institutions need public relations departments? The much-talked-about poll in *Nursing '76* (December 1976, p. 25) revealed that 38 percent of the respondents would not like to be hospitalized in their own institutions. Instead of expensive PR campaigns designed to whitewash problems and keep institutions looking good, let's work on solving the problems and making institutions better. A staff that is proud of their institution and confident of the care they give has little need for a public relations department.

Although it may seem vain and foolish to put too much emphasis on outward appearance, it is equally foolhardy to put too little emphasis on it. Plumage is important. Molloy calls the physician's short white jacket "the most powerful authority symbol in the world."

The authority conveyed by a doctor's duds can be illustrated by an amusing incident that occurred in July 1981 at John Peter Smith Hospital in Fort Worth.

During a power failure late one stormy Friday night, a young man dressed in a scrub suit stepped forward and took command of the situation. With the temperature soaring and no air conditioning available, he dispatched the staff on a late-night expedition to gather ice. They wound up with 2,000 pounds of ice in the hospital lobby. That was only one of his many *accomplishments* during the crisis.

It wasn't discovered until the wee hours of Sunday morning that the "doctor" was really a patient on the hospital's unlocked psychiatric ward.

At last we have a solution for women health professionals who don't want to be confused with the domestic staff: simply wear a short, white coat or a scrub suit. Instant respect. Instant authority. Instant power.

Although sex therapists are telling people to strip and stand naked in front of full-length mirrors, if you want to see something really revealing, try dressing for work and then standing in front of a full-length mirror. Like it or not, the clothes you wear say something about you. Among nonverbal messages, clothing speaks first. What are your clothes saying?

"I am casual."

"I am careless."

"I am professional."

"I have money."

"I am sexy."

"I had spaghetti for lunch."

Professionals in the psychiatric setting were the first to move out of uniforms and into street clothes. At one point, it was feared the staff might be competitive in trying to outdress each other. Almost the reverse occurred. Molloy stresses the importance of keeping business and leisure clothes separate. Leisure clothes say things like "Relax" or "Why work?" or "Don't take me too seriously." It might be interesting to speculate on whether the staff members' clothing compounds verbal and nonverbal messages enough to confuse patients and impede therapy.

The pediatric setting is another place where uniforms have been abandoned in favor of calico frocks that might have been designed by Mother Surrogate. I supported such changes until my own four-year-old was confronted by a pediatric resident dressed like a calypso dancer. Eric eyed him suspiciously. When the resident tried to examine him, Eric squirmed and screamed. I was alarmed, because he had never been afraid of doctors or dentists before.

When a doctor with a white jacket entered the room, Eric calmed down quickly and cooperated happily. I left wondering whether abandoning uniforms was really such a good idea. As simple-minded as it may sound, it is comforting to be able to tell the good guys from the bad guys by their garb. Instead of making children afraid of white uniforms, we may just be fostering a calico phobia.

The uniform–versus–street clothes quandary makes me think of the effect my uniform had on me when I was a student. I felt I had two distinct identities. Around the dormitory, I wore sloppy clothes and engaged in general silliness. My behavior and attitudes changed abruptly when I put on the starched white cap and uniform to go to the hospital. Technically still a teenager, I was initially surprised by the way patients bared not only their bodies but their souls. People two, three, or four times my age looked to me for comfort and guidance. My clothes made an enormous difference in the way people responded to me and, even more dramatically, in the way I responded to them.

Clothing does have a communication all its own. The next time you go to the hospital cafeteria, look around and see what wordless messages you can pick up. Wanting to display some external evidence of worth or expertise is normal. Watch for name tags with impressive titles, badges, buttons, pipes, beards, lab coats, a smattering of surgical chic, and students who conspicuously adorn their bodies with stethoscopes. (If you've got it, flaunt it!) A humorous article on the pecking order in the hospital was printed in *The Atlantic* more than 20 years ago. It is still fresh and delightful today:

Hospital hierarchy*
Marjorie Taubenhaus

In any modern hospital a pecking order, similar to that seen in bird flocks, may be observed. Of course, differences between birds and hospitals exist. Birds determine precedence simply and quickly upon meeting. They fight. The stronger bird gains for all time the right to peck the weaker. The human beings involved in a hospital situation are accustomed to use symbols as surrogates for physical combat. These symbols are usually expressed as degrees, such as M.D., R.N., or M.Sc. However, like people, once birds have established their relative rank, a peculiar, often sonorous sound, called the threat sound, may be used to maintain superiority relationships.

There is one important point of differentiation between the bird and hospital pecking orders. It lies in the ability of the birds to recognize one another. People have had to develop elaborate systems of insignia and dress to ensure the recognition of rank that is intuitively grasped by birds. The confusing multiplicity of uniforms observed in any hospital is readily understood if we know that a three hundred to four hundred bed hospital may have about a thousand persons engaged directly or indirectly with the care of patients and the running of the hospital. Most bird flocks are not this complex. The variety of dress provides a clue to the pecking order and not a functional guide for the casual visitor to the hospital.

Top man on the hospital pecking pole is the doctor. He has invested at least eight years of his life in college and medical school for the ultimate privilege of wearing a long, loose white coat. No belt in the back, it flops freely in the breeze as the physician autocratically strides down the hospital corridors. Some lucky few in every hospital wear coats threadbare and out at the elbows; these are the chiefs of service. Brown-edged acid holes, however, denote only research workers. These command no special respect except in those obscure, rarefied circles where Nobel is more than a synonym for aristocratic.

Between the long white coat and the white-jacketed medical student (stethoscope peeping coyly from his pocket) stand the intern and resident. These wear white trousers, white jackets, and white shirts, hospital issue. This costume entitles the wearer to full respect on the wards, tolerance in the semiprivate rooms, and outraged demands for a doctor from the private suites.

Although the registered nurse may not have worked through as many schools as the doctor, she has undoubtedly worked through a great many more uniforms. She achieves the final triumph of the dress-that-stands-by-itself only after progressing through the blue of the student, doffing an apron here, and picking up a cap there. Very often black lines are added to her cap and extra pins to her dress at specified and very special milestones along the

*From *The Atlantic*, vol. 203, June 1959. Copyright © 1959, by The Atlantic Monthly Company, Boston, Mass. Reprinted with permission.

way. When she has finally graduated, with the frilly headpiece chosen by the hospital of her training (as its own announcement to the world that "This nurse does things the way we do") she is then officially qualified to say "yes" to a doctor's face and "no" behind his back to everybody else in the world. The maid, the aide, the intern in his first months of training, all must turn their cheek to her peck. They may draw small comfort from the knowledge that half the starch in her uniform probably comes from the dressing down the staff doctor has just given her.

The orderly relationships of the nursing echelons are probably the most clearly defined of any in the hospital and are reflected in a veritable rainbow array of uniforms. The trained practical nurse wears white, but without a registered nurse pin, and her consequent lack of authority to dispense medications leaves her not a social leg to stand on. The student is not only in blue and white, but for the first six months of her training she is bareheaded. Once she is capped, she is well on her way up the ladder. The nurse's aide may be in green, the orderly in tan, and who can forget the Grey Lady? Order of precedence is firmly established in these variations of color and form, and a whole organization of supervisors and directors exists to protect it.

Many large urban hospitals today have social service departments, realistically as well as self-consciously important in the framework of twentieth-century medical care. On the wards the medical social worker wears a white coat, her department identified only by a nameplate on the lapel and the oddity of the coiffure above. The social worker ranks herself ostensibly just below the physician, but in truth is answerable only to God and the psychiatrist.

The hospital chef wears white in well-respected, nonmedical tradition, but he has been outmaneuvered by the dieticians. In most restaurants and hotels all over the world the high white hat of the cook represents the acme of dictatorial prestige. But the hospital dieticians have pre-empted this authority as well as a nurse's uniform. Caught in a net of calories and low-residue diets, the chef's superiority to the green-clad dishwashers is small compensation for the pecks of the nutrition experts.

Laboratory technicians circulate through the hospital in stained white coats. At feud level with the nurses, they lack the magnificent hierarchical nursing organization. Some are experts in their own fields, highly specialized and correspondingly trained. Some are just routine test runners. But the white coat covers a multitude of skills, and the technician title gives the right to a few pecks here and there.

Some few secretaries in a hospital have fought through a right to a white coat. They are the envied ones, even though they may have to suffer the slings and arrows of outrageous surgical chiefs for their dubious privilege. For, who knows? They may one day be taken for technicians.

The nether regions, both actual and rhetorical, are inhabited by a variety of persons and uniforms. Hospitals are fond of the term "ancillary personnel," and it includes the engineers, maintenance men, and laundry workers concealed in the hospital basement as well as the maids, elevator men, and pages.

The bottom of the pecking order is represented by its own, peculiarly humiliating uniform. The hospital patient, outranked by the lowliest pantry-woman, is exposed literally and figuratively in a short white chemise. This garment, barely reaching to mid-thigh, is split the length of the back and inadequately fastened at the neck and waist with strings. If a patient thinks that his position as Chairman of the Board of twenty-two large industries gives him any status, his hospital gown is calculated to dispel the delusion.

Aside from clothing, there are other nonverbal aspects that can either enhance or inhibit your attempts to be assertive. If you want to be assertive, it is nice to be tall. If you aren't tall, standing up straight will help. Posture is important. The way you carry yourself says a lot about you.

Eye contact is crucial. Keep your head up, and look the other person in the eye. If you bow your head or keep averting your eyes, your message loses much of its impact.

Body language can give you away. Nervous movements, such as swinging your foot, playing with rings, twisting your hair, biting your lip, squirming, or fidgeting, can undo your efforts to present a bold, confident, positive front. Keep hands quiet and relaxed. Don't clench or clutch.

Often it is not what you say but how you say it that counts. Stammering or groping for words does not reflect boldness. A timid, weak voice does not communicate confidence. A shrill, whining, or nagging tone can drive people away in droves. To be assertive, you need a full, well-modulated voice. Choose words carefully, and speak clearly.

Whatever the message, thought, or feeling you wish to convey to others, remember the three watchwords: bold, confident, and positive. State what you have to say frankly and concisely. Let the listener judge the content of the message independently. Don't try to prejudge, qualify, or compromise your message during delivery.

Armed with all this information, how would you handle the following situation?

A few weeks ago three of you were selected to attend your national professional convention at the hospital's expense. Not only does the convention program promise to be highly informative, it will take place in Hawaii. Hawaii! You've dreamed of going there for years.

This morning you learned that budget cutbacks mean there will be enough funding to send only one person to the convention. You desperately want to be the one chosen to go.

Sell yourself as the best candidate.
1. List four to six phrases that will help "sell" you:

_____

_____

_____

_____

2. How will your behavior be affected if:
   a. The administrator interviews each of you separately before choosing?

   _____

   _____

   b. The administrator meets with the three of you together?

   _____

   _____

3. How might you sabotage yourself? _____

   _____

   _____

This is an excellent situation to role-play or assign as a group task. Every woman needs to realize that selling herself doesn't have to mean selling others out.

We are so conditioned to be polite and to put others first that we often miss out on rare and wonderful opportunities. THE RIGHT TO ASK FOR WHAT YOU WANT is a most difficult one for women to accept. In fact, I have discovered that women hesitate to ask for what they *need*, let alone what they want.

A common error in communicating is to use negative phrasing. For example: "I don't suppose you can spare an extra nurse for our unit today." The underlying message delivered is that you really don't expect help and, therefore, you probably won't receive it. It is also a mistake to preface comments with apologetic phrases, such as "This probably isn't very important, but . . ." or "I know you hate to be bothered, but. . . ." The underlying message is that the speaker is unimportant and a bother.

When you have an important confrontation coming up, it helps to plan and rehearse. You do not need to memorize a speech word for word, but try to think of alternate phrases that express your ideas effectively. This is where an assertiveness training group can be very helpful. If you don't have a group, ask an articulate friend to listen to your ideas and help you choose suitable words and phrases. Some find practicing in front of a mirror helpful.

Behavior speaks loudly. A mother who had roomed-in with her young child during a two-week hospitalization made some interesting observations on the doctor-nurse relationship. While staying with her child all hours of the day and night, she came to know the nurses working on the unit very well. She was impressed by their wealth of knowledge and experience, their skillful guidance, and their excellent support of children and families through crises, including death. Her confidence in them grew daily, and she came to trust their judgment completely.

Because of the way she came to feel about the nurses, she found their behavior around the medical staff perplexing and irritating. Whenever the medical staff arrived, usually in bunches, the nurses would stop in the middle of whatever they were doing and retreat to a corner of the room to stand silently while the doctors talked among themselves. Rarely did the nurses volunteer information or comment on what they thought might be helpful. It was rarer still for the doctors to seek their opinions.

This quiet withdrawing of women whom she considered highly skilled and intelligent baffled her. She vividly recalled an incident when one of the doctors dropped his pen and a nurse quickly knelt to pick it up. This example seemed to sum up what she had observed over the weeks. She left vowing her daughter would never be a nurse.

Even though nurses have gotten away from standing when a doctor enters the room, the groveling reflex is still strong. Nurses keep talking about a colleague relationship with physicians, but talk is cheap. What doctors and nurses do (how they interact or fail to interact) speaks more loudly than what they say. There can never be a colleague relationship between master and servant.

Keeping us ever mindful of our lesser station in life is the environment. Our surroundings send out subtle but continuous messages. Look at the various areas of your institution. You can assess the importance of the people occupying them by the amount of space, quality of furnishings, and depth of carpeting.

Have you ever been ushered into the doctors' conference room or the room where the board of directors meets once a month? The setting is plush. Contrast that with the conference space available to the bulk of hospital employees. Most women are grateful for a vacated broom closet. We are glad to have any place where we can spend a few uninterrupted moments discussing and planning patient care.

For an environmental message reflecting the institution's view of your value, go to the women employees' locker room. One interior decorator does hospital locker rooms nationwide. The walls are invariably painted with an unusual pastel shade somewhere between blah and yuck. The paint industry manages to mistakenly mix about 4,000 gallons each year and then distributes it wholesale to institutions at twice what a normal color would cost. The furniture has all the warmth of cheap plastic and comes in a variety of gaudy colors accentuated by masking tape over splits and tears. Completing the decor are corroded plumbing fixtures and mosaic tile floors with random pieces missing. The atmosphere is enhanced by a heavy pine-scented disinfectant splashed liberally by the housekeeping department, whose members can barely tolerate being in the room long enough to do minimal upkeep. The room is a marvelous place to relax, take a break, converse with friends, and confer with colleagues.

Many nurses are still required to punch time clocks. This minor ritual keeps the nursing staff guessing about their professional status and chips away at an inflated idea they may have about their self-worth. The subtle implication is that management cannot trust nurses to do an honest day's work. Working with sick people, however, is not as predictable as assembly-line work, and overtime begins to pile up. Management regrets they cannot compensate for overtime but feels that the nursing staff—as a professional group—must realize patient care cannot be regulated by a clock. Confusing, isn't it?

Bombarded with put-downs from the environment and management, it is no wonder we have difficulty salvaging our self-esteem. Our attire, working conditions, salary, lack of access to policy-making boards, and pervasive powerlessness add up to a domestic image instead of a professional one.

Although the domestic image may be difficult to avoid, the domestic mentality—dull, plodding, unquestioning, subservient—is something women health professionals are finding easier to refuse. We are skilled. We are intelligent. We are the majority.

Early in his career the famous architect Frank Lloyd Wright said he had to choose between honest arrogance and hypocritical humility. He chose the former. Isn't it time we permitted ourselves a little honest arrogance and reveled in unabashed, unashamed appreciation of the talents, skills, and experiences that have made us the professionals we are today?

The time has come to make the silent majority visible. No more timid titmouse. It is a shame Patient Protector is just a figment of the imagination. We could use a role model with a dash more flair, imagination, and daring to help us shed the dowdy plumage assigned to those who are bland, conservative, and methodical.

Maybe we should all show up for work wearing Patient Protector costumes. Initially, the administration might mistake us for clowns, but they would soon learn that this is no laughing matter. Women constitute more than 85 percent of the health service work force. We have the right to be recognized, to be taken seriously, and to share in making any decisions or policies that affect patient care or our jobs.

Image is an issue too long ignored by women in the health professions. As individuals we may be invisible, but if we ever unite, there would be a tidal wave on that subservient sea of white that could forever alter the present health care system, if not sweep it away entirely.

9
Pigeons

Want your fortune, Cookie?

To borrow and bend a phrase from P.T. Barnum, there's a pigeon born every minute, and at least half of them are women. Pigeons are people who are a little too naive, a little too gullible, a little too trusting.

For all the pigeons out there, I have some good news and some bad news. The bad news is that the world is full of manipulators, both malignant and benign. The good news is that people can only manipulate you if you let them. You can't blame a guy for trying. You have the option to say no.

Although you are surrounded by people who are ready, willing, and able to take advantage of you, not all of them are malicious. Most of them are just trying to get a job done and see you as a means of accomplishing their task. This applies to the persistent potato-peeler salesman as well as the parish priest.

Several times a day you may be tested to see how much work or worry you are willing to give to a cause. Like most women you may be a giver, but after a while you tire of making sacrifices, doing extra duty, missing social functions, being expected to always come through in a pinch, and settling for a pat on the back instead of an increase in your paycheck.

When your sense of humor and sunny disposition begin to fade, you have given enough. The time has come to look at how your life is being spent. Are you spending your life, or is someone else always borrowing it and spending it for you?

For some people time is money. For all of us time is life. Unlike a cup of sugar, time borrowed can never be returned.

Look at those around you, and think about how you take advantage of them. If you want something done for you, how do you approach others? Think about the people you usually ask for favors. Someone quipped, "If you can't take advantage of your friends, whom can you take advantage of?"

Vacation

This year you have made elaborate plans for your vacation. Reservations were completed almost three months ago. You are eagerly counting the few remaining days until you leave.

This morning you are called to your supervisor's office and told that the other head nurse on your floor has just resigned — effective immediately.

Supervisor: "I know your vacation was to begin Monday, but you can see what a terrible bind we're in! I hate to impose, but you are the only person who could possibly manage both units at once. Mary's resignation certainly was a shock — so irresponsible. I'm glad I've always been able to count on you."

How would you respond?

1. Physical response: _____

2. Emotional response: _____

3. Verbal response:

a. What I would like to say to her is, "_____

_____."

b. But, a more effective thing to say is, "_____

_____."

The best way to keep people from taking advantage of you and using your life is to be able to recognize the ploys likely to be used against you. Here are a few to consider.

Flattery. Women's work is so often taken for granted that you may not only be hungry for praise or recognition, you may be starving. It's hard to keep your head when a sweet talker comes along cooing, "You are the only person I can really talk to" or "You are the best nurse on the floor."

Whenever you find yourself being buttered up, beware: chances are you are about to be manipulated. Accept compliments graciously, but resist the compulsion to return a compliment or to comply with the flatterers' requests just because you want to keep their esteem. If their esteem is that shallow, it isn't worth keeping.

Criticism. This ploy is the opposite of flattery but just as effective. If flattery fails, criticism may quickly follow in its footsteps. Even a slight implication that you are a bad mother, an inadequate wife, or an insensitive therapist can cut you to the bone. All the NOT OK feelings suddenly surface. You begin to doubt yourself again. Perhaps you are not as wise or wonderful, as competent or compassionate as you thought. Perhaps you are being selfish or illogical.

Acceptance of your own nonperfect self is not a one-time conquest. You may have to deal with it again. Give yourself time to sort through critical remarks. Remember to consider their content and their intent. Consider the source. Do not make any long-range plans, sweeping changes in your lifestyle, or coerced commitments when you are feeling down on yourself.

Insecurity. A would-be manipulator makes good use of your fears. For example, the underlying fear that you can always be replaced may make you take on all kinds of extra tasks so that your family or employer will see how indispensable you are. Soon the extra tasks are absorbed into the standard expectations. To keep winning the irreplaceable title, you have to take on more and more tasks, until you buckle under the load.

A mere hint that love is about to be withdrawn makes many women hastily comply with a manipulator's demands. If you are terrified at the prospect of being left alone, it is time you got to know yourself and like yourself better. Only then will you be able to withstand such a cowardly and cruel attack.

Fear of what people will think exerts a lot of control over your behavior.

This fear keeps you searching for the straight and narrow road supposedly trod by good mothers, good wives, good neighbors, good customers, good therapists, good whatevers. Unfortunately, this road is so nebulous that even a good whatever is likely to have a nervous breakdown trying to follow it.

When anticipating how assertiveness will look on you, it is natural to ask, "What will people think?" The answer is simply: "People will think anything they please." You have no control over other people's thoughts. It is what you think that is important. Don't be too quick to alter your behavior on the basis of what people might think. Their thoughts are unpredictable.

Fear of offending someone—anyone!—keeps many women from being assertive. If a manipulator is offended when you refuse to comply, just hum the line from the popular song that goes, "You can't please everyone, so you've got to please yourself."

Our insecurity gives manipulators excellent leverage to use against us. Insecurity can be highly profitable. For example, women have spent millions of dollars on feminine deodorant products that have been shown to be virtually useless and potentially harmful. (Ever wonder why masculine deodorant products aren't on the market?)

Your assignment for today is to think about the things you have done and the products you have purchased because you weren't secure enough to refuse or resist.

Helplessness. The old what-would-I-do-without-you routine capitalizes on your need to be needed. The corporate tycoon who can't straighten his tie or remember his appointments somehow manages to make millions. His secretary, like all other unsung heroines, is content to stay in the background, poor but secure in the knowledge that he couldn't do it without her.

Women often foster helpless behavior in others and then complain and condemn that same behavior. A husband may be all thumbs at cooking or cleaning, so the wife takes over those chores again. The husband sighs, "Well, I tried." The wife is again overworked but temporarily more content, because she has proved once again that he couldn't manage without her.

Resist the urge to rush in and take over someone else's work just because he or she appears helpless or because you know you can do it faster. All of us have strengths that outnumber our weaknesses. Husbands and children can be helpful instead of helpless. It just takes practice, patience, and praise.

Obligation. It's your duty as a citizen (nurse, mother, Christian) to do this, that, and the other thing. Women have been made to feel responsible for the welfare and happiness of others. That's a tall order. Ensuring welfare is difficult; ensuring happiness is impossible.

Obviously, you do have obligations to your husband, children, employer, and others. What is often overlooked is that these people have obligations to you also. Agreeing to share your life with others brings obligations that differ from those which accompany agreeing to give your life to others.

When you feel bogged down by things you "ought" to do or "should" do, rethink your priorities and obligations. You have no obligation to strive for sainthood or martyrdom. Martyrs are for burning.

Guilt. This sister of obligation is the ultimate weapon in the manipulator's arsenal. Feelings of guilt are powerful persuaders that are easily evoked and perhaps more difficult to deal with than any other emotion. Guilt is cunning, merciless, and usually Number One on the hit parade.

> "It will break your mother's heart if you don't come home for Christmas."
> "Thousands of people are starving to death, and you won't eat what's on your plate."
> "You should be grateful just to be alive."
> "If you really loved me, you would do as I ask."
> "How can you refuse to help the poor and needy?"

Guilt comes in twinges and torrents. Whenever you begin feeling guilty, stop and examine what is happening to you. Guilt can become a way of life. Some women even feel guilty about feeling good.

When you are knee-deep in guilt, you are susceptible to all types of manipulation and may agree to do things as a form of self-punishment, a kind of penance for sins real or imagined. Wait for guilt to subside before making any agreements or commitments.

• • •

After being taken advantage of or being used, your predominant feeling is anger. Unresolved anger will corrode stomach linings as well as friendships. Be assured that angry people *always* respond, either outwardly or inwardly.

If you swallow your anger, you have a choice of headaches, ulcers, asthma attacks, back problems, dermatitis, fatigue, insomnia, nerves, and more. Write your own favorite malady here: _____. If you spit your anger out, you may spit on the wrong person. You may be tempted to use others as you have been used.

An amateur manipulator doesn't stand a chance against a professional manipulator. When pigeons use these tactics to retaliate, they often backfire. Pigeons may resort to devious, indirect methods of getting even. Do any of the following sound familiar?

Bitching. Frustrated people do a lot of complaining, griping, backbiting, gossiping, and nagging. Although this is a common response to being used, it is ineffective and more likely to foster tension than relieve it.

Ignoring. When someone asks for help or tries to get you to fetch something, you turn a deaf ear. You try not to acknowledge the other person's presence and may even walk out of the room while he is talking to you.

Sniping. In this form of guerrilla warfare, you take potshots at the big shots, hoping to cut them down to size. Sarcasm is a near-lethal weapon if you have a sharp wit and tongue to match. You can be blunt and hurtful in the name of honesty.

Forgetting. "Oops, I forgot." An angry person can easily forget to call Mother, miss committee meetings, fail to keep a doctor's appointment, or leave errands undone.

Procrastinating. A person might agree to cooperate but neglect responsibilities for so long that someone else has to do the task.

Lateness. Being chronically slow or late holds others up, making everyone anxious and irritated. This can also be used by people who want to make a grand entrance.

Sabotage. This is the neat trick of doing work so poorly that you will not be asked to do it again. All it takes is a little carelessness or poor timing.

•   •   •

Pigeons know these behaviors are childish and petty. (If they don't know, a professional manipulator will be quick to point this out.) After a while, they begin to despise their actions and end up feeling even more foolish, incompetent, and guilty. The net result is a lowered self-esteem, and with a lower self-esteem, the pigeon is even more open to manipulation.

As a woman and a health worker, what are the ploys that have been used against you? Are you more sensitive to approaches through flattery, criticism, insecurity, helplessness, obligation, or guilt? Can you recognize manipulators and manipulation? Can you handle both without feeling angry, bitter, or foolish?

A major goal of assertiveness is to help you discharge anger without going to the extremes of either homicide or suicide. The first step toward resolution is to stop running away. Give yourself permission to be angry. Don't deny and try to hide your true feelings. The next step is to face the person making you miserable. (You may need a mirror to do this.) You have to be willing to look and listen, to acknowledge the other person's presence, along with his feelings and opinions. Acknowledgment does not mean agreement.

Who's in charge here?

"When Katherine returned to our organization after an extended absence, she was offered her old management position back but turned it down. I was offered the position and accepted.

> On this particular occasion I made a scheduling decision and then went to lunch. When I returned she had changed everything involved in my decision and ordered other things done.
>
> I was new in this job and had less work experience in this area than she did. I was so angry I couldn't react rationally. I did nothing. When the day was over, I went home frustrated, angry, crying, and wanting to do grave bodily harm to someone."

Even if Katherine slipped into her old role unconsciously, she should be alerted to her inappropriate behavior. If she did it maliciously, she needs to be dealt with swiftly. Both of you need to clarify your present and future roles.

You will save yourself a lot of grief if you confront her immediately: "I was surprised (shocked, upset, appalled) to see that you changed my scheduling decision." Then wait calmly for her explanation.

If you absolutely cannot deal with her immediately, it is not too late to be assertive tomorrow. Take her aside and say, "I see a potential problem developing and I want to discuss it with you. Yesterday, when I returned from lunch and found you had changed my scheduling decision, I was so angry I couldn't discuss it. I want to discuss it now."

If her explanation is unsatisfactory or if you fear this may become a repetitive problem, be firm: "While I welcome your input and value your advice, it is my responsibility now to make these decisions. Once I decide, my decision stands."

The following is a very similar situation in which assertiveness was put to the test:

> "I became evening charge nurse replacing an older nurse who had been demoted after 20 years of service. The staff continued to seek her out to solve problems and make decisions. Finally, I called a meeting of all personnel and told them I was the charge nurse now and I expected to have the problems brought directly to me. Oddly enough, the situation improved tremendously."

It wasn't odd at all. Assertiveness works.

To stop being a pigeon, it is crucial to know what your weaknesses are, because that is where the manipulators will strike first. But a second line of defense is needed in a place where you would least expect it. If the sophisticated manipulators cannot reach you through your weaknesses, they will use your strengths against you.

It has been said that a product's greatest strength is also its greatest weakness. That's a handy thing to remember when a salesman comes knocking at your door. If he praises his product because it is plastic, lightweight, and inexpensive, you can be sure that those advantages are also its disadvantages.

You may wish to reconsider that plastic is nonporous, rigid, tends to crack under pressure and is difficult to patch or repair. Lightweight? Then it cannot be very substantial or stable. By now you know that you cannot get something for nothing, so if it is inexpensive, costs had to be cut in materials, labor, or design.

In the same manner, a person's greatest strengths may also be used as weaknesses. Take another look at the list you prepared in Chapter 2. Check your strengths and think about how they may be used against you.

Are you a hard worker? Good, then fewer of you have to be hired.

Are you dedicated? Good, then you can be paid less.

Are you concerned, caring, and compassionate? Good, then you will find it difficult to ask for a raise or a day off, to refuse to work rotating shifts, overtime, holidays, or weekends.

Are you dependable? Good, then you won't need much attention.

Religious? Good, then you know all about giving being better than receiving and turning the other cheek.

Married? Good, then you don't need a job that can support you, and you will probably get pregnant before you get a promotion or a raise.

Responsible? Good, then you'll take the blame.

Just as some people are professional manipulators, others are professional pigeons. In the health field alone, there are more than 3 million of us.

Women in the health professions are often taken advantage of in the name of sweet charity. Our salaries can be summed up in three words: cheap, cheap, cheap. "The mass of the health care workers receive salaries which are eight to twenty percent of those earned by salaried physicians."*

For years we have literally donated our time and talent, believing we were doing so in the service of others. As the injustices and inequities of our health care system become more apparent, some of us are beginning to feel less like angels of mercy and more like accomplices in crime.

Whereas the quality of health care seems to be slipping, the cost of that care is skyrocketing. Coming from middle and lower socioeconomic backgrounds, women health workers know the value of a dollar. We have been highly sensitized to the fact that any increase in our pay, however slight, will be passed along to patients. We have been made to feel guilty for even thinking that we should be financially compensated for our education, work experience, or level of responsibility.

One of the biggest hoaxes ever perpetrated on the American public is that health care is a nonprofit service. Health care is big business. No industry that

---

*Rodrigues-Trios, Helen: Proceedings of the International Conference on Women in Health, Washington, D.C., June 16-18, 1975, Department of Health, Education, and Welfare, p. 164.

collects $272 million a day, $99.6 billion a year, should be classified as nonprofit. The expenses are huge, but so are the profits. These profits have been siphoned off into the hands of a chosen few: pill producers, building contractors, equipment manufacturers, insurance companies, and physicians. For these people, health care is not a service; it is a bonanza. It is nonprofit only for pigeons and patients.

Health care in the United States can literally be a crime. In Wisconsin, one physician was investigated because it was estimated that he would have had to make a house call every 15 minutes, seven days a week, 365 days a year to justify the money he collected from the government through Medicare. It is much safer than to stick up a gas station. Who is going to stick up for us?

Women in the health professions wouldn't mind giving if there weren't so many on the take. Most of us would continue working for peanuts because we honestly care about patients. Money is not the cause of unrest in our ranks. The cause is power. We don't have any.

Many women fear power because of its negative connotations. They picture vindictive, power-mad Amazons whose motto is "Today, the health care industry. Tomorrow, the world!" The power being discussed here is more analogous to electricity: the spark needed to make things move, to get things done. Power to bring energy and light into the health care system. Women have been unplugged too long.

Although men have delegated a lot of responsibility to women, they have not delegated the necessary authority to go with it. If power corrupts and absolute power corrupts absolutely, women are incorruptible. In almost every phase of government, industry, and education, women have no power, no clout. In the health care industry, this inequity is even more obvious and more ludicrous. More than 80 percent of health care workers are women; yet only about 2 percent of the top echelons of doctors, health department officials, and administrators are women.*

> Although the women may *do* most of the work, the doctors and hospital administrators have control over the work, make the decisions, tell other workers what to do. The role of most women in the American medical system, even women in supervisory capacities, is to work *for* the bureaucracy, for the doctors and the hospitals. Most workers' primary task is to serve the needs of the doctors and hospitals, and only secondarily to serve the needs of the patients. The bureaucratic superiors not only control the subordinate workers but also control the interaction of the patients with the workers. Although most women in health service see themselves as helping patients, and went into health work for that purpose, the actual decisions they can make and the

*Rodriguez-Trios, op. cit., p. 164.

actions they can take are controlled from above. They are taught in training programs and on the job that they should not take independent action, they should not make decisions, they should not challenge their superiors. In short, they should know their place.*

The nursing profession is actively engaged in a struggle for some influence or control over working conditions and patient-care policies. The American Nurses' Association, which represents about 200,000 nurses in the United States, has been seeking membership on a national council that accredits "nursing" homes and other long-term care facilities. Consistently voting against nurses' membership are the American Medical Association and the American Health Care Association. (Ironically, AHCA's former title was the American *Nursing* Home Association.)

According to Thelma M. Schorr, editor of the *American Journal of Nursing*, the Joint Commission on Accreditation of Hospitals (parent body of the AHCA)

> has been playing a funny doctor-nurse, cat-and-mouse game with the ANA for more than 25 years. It seeks nursing consultation, employs nurses and uses them liberally on its accrediting teams, frequently seeks ANA input on its various documents, offers representation on a variety of committees—and then pulls back sharply when the request for full membership representation with voting rights is made.†

Five years have passed. ANA still does not have voting rights. And we thought women's suffrage was settled decades ago!

Like most bureaucratic blimps, the commission continues to float miles above the real world, issuing decisions that directly and profoundly affect patient care and those who give it. The people closest to the patients and the problems, those who have to deal face to face, day after day, struggling to cope and hoping improvements are on the way, are not allowed to vote.

The ANA has behaved in an assertive manner, persistently petitioning for the right to participate and share in responsibility for health care facilities. If resistance from physicians and businessmen continues, and there is no reason to think it will not, further steps must be taken.

The time has come to speak up. Not to speak up to the commission (the ANA has tried that for years), but to make our case known to the general public. Never underestimate the power of the press. The consumer is a potentially strong but sleeping ally who is slowly beginning to wake up to a variety of health care rip-offs.

---

*Brown, Carol A.: Proceedings of the International Conference on Women in Health, Washington, D.C., June 16-18, 1975, Department of Health, Education, and Welfare, p. 150.
†Schorr, Thelma M.: Editorial, Am. J. Nurs. **77**:53, 1977.

Just saying "nursing home" makes most people shudder. Why not let newspapers and magazines know that we are sick and tired of having the good name of nursing besmirched by the deplorable and scandalous conditions found in "nursing" homes. Let them know that many of these facilities employ only the token nurses required by law, making it clear that "nursing home" is a misnomer. Since most of these "homes" are owned and operated by physicians or businessmen, it seems only fair that they be called "doctoring" homes or "businessing" homes . . . or parking lots—anything but "nursing" homes!

Women need to regain some of the spunk and spirit they had in the past. For instance, during the late 1800s women owned and operated medical colleges and hospitals of their own because admission to medical schools was denied them. According to Mary Roth Walsh, author of *Doctors Wanted: No Women Need Apply: Sexual Barriers in the Medical Profession 1835-1975,*[*] the turn of the century was a "golden age" for women doctors. In 1900 more than 18 percent of Boston's physicians were women. That figure has not been surpassed to this day.

Eventually, resourcefulness appeared to pay off, and women were granted entrance to the nation's medical schools. By 1894 women represented a significant portion of the student body: as much as 37 percent at Boston University. Believing their battle for sexual equality in medicine had been won, women's rights advocates shifted their attention elsewhere. Convinced that they had outlived their usefulness, 19 separate women's medical colleges closed their doors.

Almost immediately, male physicians declared concern that a surplus of doctors was developing, and they not only reduced enrollments but managed to limit the number of women to 4 or 5 percent of each class. Walsh cautions that a similar backlash against women medical students could develop again today. She notes that, although there have been substantial gains, the number of women in influential positions remains unchanged. Medical schools and hospitals have refused to appoint women to key leadership positions.

One alternative might be for women to again own and operate institutions themselves. A better alternative might be to make every effort to bypass bureaucracy and institutions altogether.

Muriel Sieh, a social worker in Phoenix, Arizona, is an excellent example of assertiveness in action. Her father had been in several unsatisfactory nursing homes. Finally, she found a supportive family that could give him the care he needed. In three weeks, he began to gain weight, and his monthly medical bills dropped to less than one-fourth their former level.

Convinced she could do this for others as well, she developed the Arizona

---

*New Haven, Conn., 1977, Yale University Press.

Adult Foster Home Registry. The foster homes are located through civic and social groups. Depending on the special care needed, boarders are charged from $150 to $600 per month. In the registry's first two years of operation, 60 residents found a pleasing alternative to nursing homes or hospitals.

With some imagination and boldness, we might be able to dream up all kinds of alternatives. My favorite health care fantasy is inspired by a mental health institute that charges between $70 and $120 per day. At these rates, the patients should have satin sheets and filet mignon and see Sigmund Freud himself twice a week. Instead, they receive custodial care and are lucky to see a resident who speaks pidgin English once a month. I often think it would be cheaper and more therapeutic to give chronic schizophrenics 90-day passes on Greyhound bus lines and let them stay at Holiday Inn. Don't be afraid to let your imagination run wild. You couldn't possibly dream up any system more outlandish, inefficient, or expensive than the one we already have.

Future trends are bound to take health care out of institutions and back into the home. We cannot afford to do otherwise. When it comes to health care, women are still willing to deliver. Women health workers are already moving out into the community to support families who want to be together during important moments such as when someone is being born or when someone is dying.

Perhaps women should begin to take their business elsewhere. Hit the health industry where it hurts—in the pocketbook. Once we might have been gullible enough to believe that herding people into institutions would result in cheaper, better care. But no more.

If professional women have been pigeons, women patients have been sitting ducks. There is recent and growing evidence that the sexist practices in medicine are hazardous to women's health.

In *The Hidden Malpractice*, Gena Corea calls attention to the fact that hysterectomies have become the most frequently performed major surgery in the United States and are often done without valid medical reason. When surgeons know their practices are being studied, the percentage of "unjustified" hysterectomies drops by two thirds.

Millions of women are taking contraceptive pills or wearing intrauterine devices, even though both pose some medical risks. Meanwhile, efforts to develop a male contraceptive have lagged.

Male-dominated childbirth is being questioned. It is well documented that U.S. infant mortality levels remain well above those of many countries where midwives attend births. Writing in *Immaculate Deception: A New Look at Women and Childbirth in America*,* Suzanne Arms notes that the

---

*New York, 1977, Bantam Books, Inc.

number of Cesarean births has doubled in recent years, with some hospitals recording 30 percent of births by this method.

Psychiatry's attitude toward women is also suspect. For instance, an inordinate number of lobotomies have been performed on female as opposed to male psychiatric patients. Sociologist Richard Levinson observes:

> Returning a female to a traditionally passive, dependent role as housewife-domestic is less difficult to accomplish than enabling a male to return to an occupational position requiring technical skills, creativity, or high intelligence. Psychosurgeons looking for impressive outcomes do well to prefer the aged and women.*

Whereas physicians see men as having real illnesses, they see women's illnesses as primarily psychosomatic and are twice as likely to prescribe a mood-altering drug for a woman than for a man.

> Almost half of American women (45 percent) use such drugs regularly. . . . Women are an astonishing 70 percent of the habitual users of minor tranquilizers and 72 percent of the antidepressant users.†

As professionals and as patients, women have been too trusting. We have assumed that men were looking out for our best interests. It appears we assumed too much.

After several deaths of women on a liquid protein diet were reported, the diet's author was interviewed on national television. It was pointed out to him that all the women had been under medical supervision. His reply was, "There is medical supervision, and then there is medical supervision."

Slowly but surely, women are becoming less gullible, less obedient. We are beginning to be more assertive in seeking health care, in valuing second opinions, in reading and researching illnesses and medications. The publication of *Our Bodies, Ourselves*‡ was a landmark in helping us understand our bodies enough to seek informed medical care.

Seeking medical care and seeking health care are two entirely different things. Unfortunately, the terms are so often used interchangeably that they are assumed to be synonymous. But medical care is care given by physicians, whereas health care encompasses the valuable services rendered by dietitians, psychologists, pharmacists, dentists, nurses, physical therapists, and others in addition to doctors.

When the term "physician extender" was introduced, all I could think of was grinding up soybeans to make sirloin go farther. Personally, I don't enjoy

---

*Levinson, Richard: Sexism in nursing, Am. J. Nurs. **76**:430, 1976.
†Corea, Gena: The hidden malpractice, New York, 1977, Jove Publications, Inc. p. 92.
‡Boston Women's Health Book Collective, New York, 1973, Simon & Schuster, Inc.

being thought of as the soy of life. Although I wouldn't object to being called a "health care extender," I find "physician extender" offensive.

Many doctors are very good at what they do, but what they do is more limited than anyone is willing to admit. It is estimated that 75 percent of all symptoms are not related to any organic disease but to tension, depression, frustration, loneliness, lack of coping skills, poor interpersonal relationships, and so forth. No amount of surgery or drugs can correct these problems. Read the *Journal of the American Medical Association* and you will find its content almost exclusively related to organic disease. Doctors concentrate on tissue damage, not on damage to the individual or the family.

Furthermore, it is estimated that 20 percent of all patients in a typical research hospital acquire an iatrogenic disease.* *Iatrogenic*. Sounds like a new virus, but it means "physician-induced." Translated, that means that 20 percent of the patients have to be treated for problems resulting from medical treatment itself.

Finally, women are beginning to question whether the team concept is viable in our present system. Our health care system has never been a democracy. It is a dictatorship. It might best be compared with a game in which the child who owns the ball refuses to play unless the others agree to play by his rules and his rules alone. Under such circumstances, even if a team is organized, it can never be a winning one.

Perhaps it was a mistake to admit women to institutions of higher learning. The more we learn, the less we understand. We do not understand why our salaries, fringe benefits, and advancement opportunities should be less than those of men. Even more important, we do not understand why we are allowed no voice and no vote in the policies and practices of the health care industry. We pigeons have toed the line long enough.

In closing this chapter, let us all stand and sing the rousing "Battle Hymn of Uppity Nurses" (p. 102).

---

*Illich, Ivan: Medical nemesis, New York, 1976, Bantam Books, Inc., p. 23.

BATTLE HYMN OF UPPITY NURSES

Words: Melodie Chenevert
*Music: Slightly borrowed.**

I joined the health professions
To fight pain and misery
But after my 8 hours
I'm the one in agony
So much to do, so little time
It really is a shame—
And I'm the one they blame

Chorus
Don't let the health industry screw ya
Get what you've got coming to ya
The quality of care will soon unglue ya
If the patient's just a pawn

I worked on Christmas, New Years
Thanksgiving and Halloween
I'm not sure but I think I had
A weekend in between
Rotating shifts and lack of help

Can make a person mean—
When the patient's just a pawn

Reporting off I wished the next shift
"Bon voyage, good luck!"
We've 17 on critical
And 12 IV's are stuck
The resident is deaf and dumb
The laundry's gone amuck—
And the patient's just a pawn

I work hard as any surgeon
But I rarely hear a "thanks"
I'm still saving for support hose
He's got money in Swiss banks
If you think that this is quite unfair
Then come and join our ranks—
Or the patient's just a pawn

---

*To be sung to the tune, "Battle Hymn of the Republic," sometimes better known as "Glory, Glory, Hallelujah." Should be accompanied by kazoos or the local philharmonic—whichever is cheaper.

From barnyard to mountaintop

It takes more than hot air to make
dreams come true.

The Colorado Nurses' Association once called to see if I could give a workshop on "advanced assertiveness." Being very bold, confident, and positive, I assured them I could. Frankly, at that moment I didn't know what advanced assertiveness was, but if I couldn't find it, I would invent it. (Some shameless people will do anything to get out of the barnyard and up to mountaintops as beautiful as those in Vail, Colorado.)

Even before I hung up the phone, I was mentally trying to differentiate between basic and advanced assertiveness. While I worked on the problem, four categories or levels of assertiveness began to take shape. They crystallized into remedial assertiveness, basic assertiveness, advanced assertiveness, and beyond assertiveness (Table 1).

Remedial assertiveness. Table 1 can be read both vertically and horizontally. To help clarify the material condensed there, let's begin with a verbal sketch of the woman who is in need of remedial assertiveness training. First and foremost, she has little or no self-esteem. Feeling inadequate in most of life's arenas, she frequently belittles her ability, education, talent, and experience.

Her prime directive is to avoid conflict at all costs. That's why she is so reluctant to use the word "no." Saying no to someone causes conflict. Quiet, obedient, and conforming, she allows and even depends on others to tell her what to do and where to go.

Although there are many things she really doesn't want to do, she does them anyway. "If I don't do it, no one else will," she sighs. It never occurs to her that if she is the *only* person willing to do something, perhaps it is not worth doing.

A martyr in the making, she tends to be self-sacrificing and masochistic. She tries to use guilt to control others, even as she is controlled by it. Having resigned herself to making do with whatever is available, she would not presume to ask for what she needs, let alone what she wants. Seeing herself as a victim of fate (culture, sex, time, space), she feels powerless to make changes in her life. She has dreams but few aspirations and no goals.

She is a nice person, a polite person. She is also fearful, depressed, and very tired. Blinded by anxiety, she sees no alternatives. She simply does what she is told and wishes everyone else would do the same.

To help her venture even close to the borderline that separates passive from assertive behavior will require weeks, months, or perhaps years of gentle coaching and systematic, sympathetic support.

Basic assertiveness. Contrast the woman at the remedial assertiveness stage with the one who has achieved a basic assertiveness level in theory and practice. Here is a woman who has begun to value her time, talent, education, and experience. Her budding self-esteem is fragile but growing stronger each day.

Handling uncomplicated conflicts with waiters, clerks, mechanics, and virtual strangers is a snap. She has even been known to confront some people in high places like her boss, minister, and husband. Busy testing old relationships, values, and stereotypes, she enjoys flexing her newfound mental, physical, and emotional muscles.

Suddenly aware that alternatives exist, she begins weighing choices, making changes, and taking chances. She devotes time and energy to plans and activities that will enhance *her* personal and professional life.

In many ways it is a selfish time. After years of passive, cooperative behavior in which she has ignored her own needs and catered to the wants and wishes of others, she begins putting herself first. When asked to do chores and tasks that she doesn't want to do, she refuses. She refuses with almost sadistic glee.

For the woman at this level, assertiveness is more likely to be used as a weapon than a tool. Her attitude and behavior changes often confuse and alienate those around her. Although she is not as easily affected by guilt, she is not immune to it either.

This rather negative but necessary phase is disruptive and uncomfortable. So uncomfortable that the weak may retreat and return to passiveness . . . and Valium. Others, too aware to return to old attitudes and behaviors, yet too fearful or shortsighted to push ahead, accept the elementary gains of basic assertiveness. They are content with what they have learned in Assertiveness 101. However, the strong and those blessed with support and encouragement continue exploring, exercising, and experimenting with assertiveness. They are the ones who will go on to advanced assertiveness.

Advanced assertiveness. To reach this third level of assertiveness, a woman must outgrow the depression of the first level and the anger of the second. She has to make the critical connection between assertiveness and achievement.

The woman who masters advanced assertiveness has high regard for her own time, talent, education, and experience. Not only does she have definite personal and professional goals, she also has workable plans to achieve them. Having assimilated assertiveness, she uses it skillfully to save time and energy and to move forward toward her goals. She is a woman who knows what she wants and is no longer afraid to go after it.

Unlike a woman at a lower level of assertiveness who floats adrift at the mercy of people, places, and events (external locus of control), the woman at a higher level of assertiveness takes charge of her life. She operates from an

TABLE 1. **FOUR LEVELS OF ASSERTIVENESS**

REMEDIAL ASSERTIVENESS	**BASIC ASSERTIVENESS**	**ADVANCED ASSERTIVENESS**	**BEYOND ASSERTIVENESS**
Has low self-esteem	Has budding self-esteem	Has high self-esteem plus high esteem for others	Is willing to take risks personally and professionally
Is afraid to say no	Delights in saying no	Is comfortable saying no—delights in saying yes	
Masochistic	*Sadistic*	*Holistic*	
Avoids conflict at all costs	Handles uncomplicated conflict comfortably	Recognizes conflict as potentially positive; enjoys seeking resolution	
Anxiety	*Action*	*Energy*	*Power*
Knows what she doesn't want but does it anyway	Knows what she doesn't want and refuses to do it	Knows what she wants . . . and is not afraid to go for it!	
Dependent	*Independent*	*Interdependent*	
Sees no alternatives	Is aware alternatives exist	Chooses from alternatives	Invents alternatives
Conformity		*Creativity*	
Lacks direction	Seeks direction	Is self-directed	Shares direction

	Needs support	Self-supporting	Supports others
	Seeks	Is sought by others	
	External locus of control		Internal locus of control
	Won't do	Can do	
Hides			
Makes do			

MASLOW

Individual	Communal	National	Global
Followership		**Leadership**	**Fellowship**
Is cowardly	Is curious	Is confident	
Plans hourly/daily	Plans monthly/yearly	Plans three/five/ten years ahead	Plans for lifetime and beyond
Lets others define goals	Defines personal goals	Has definite goals and workable plans for achieving them	Continually formulates, updates, redefines, and prioritizes goals
Considers personal time, talent, education, and experience inadequate	Begins to value personal time, talent, education, and experience	Has high regard for personal time, talent, education, and experience	Values time, talent, education, and experience of others

internal locus of control. She makes decisions. She takes chances. She acts instead of reacts.

When conflict arises, she sees it as potentially positive and actually enjoys challenges. Willingly she takes responsibility for her actions and their consequences. She makes significant choices and leaves little to chance.

Hardworking, energetic, and self-reliant, she radiates confidence. Although she is comfortable saying no, she delights in saying yes. In contrast to the first-level woman who "makes do" and the second-level woman who "won't do," her motto is "Can do!"

Beyond assertiveness. Just as the transition from remedial to basic assertiveness is long and difficult, getting from basic to advanced assertiveness requires another quantum jump. Once at the advanced level, however, it is merely a gradual slide into the fourth level. Perhaps "beyond assertiveness" is more of an extension than a level of its own.

At this point the woman incorporates all the attributes, attitudes, and actions previously discussed and more. High self-esteem is vital, but so is high esteem for others. The woman at this level is a powerful person in the most positive sense of the word. A high achiever in her own right, she also *enables* others to do their best work by maximizing their strenghts instead of lingering on their limitations. Encounters with her leave others energized, not drained.

Positive and adventurous in her approach, the woman of beyond assertiveness is willing to take risks both personally and professionally. She not only chooses from alternatives, she also invents them. She creates jobs, markets, products, solutions, manuscripts. Innovation is her hallmark.

Her planning includes her lifetime and beyond. Much of what she is working on or for will benefit her children, grandchildren, and great-grandchildren. She is continually formulating, updating, redefining, and prioritizing her goals.

• • •

As you consider these four levels of assertiveness, try to identify the level at which you entered the continuum, the level you have attained, and the level you would like to master. Are you growing in assertiveness or just thrashing around?

Don't be impatient. The metamorphosis from chicken to eagle takes time. If you are not quite ready to leave the barnyard for the mountaintop, at least hop on top of the chicken coop and see what is going on around you.

It may be lonely at the top, but it's crowded at the bottom. With each technical advance and each new service or pseudoservice, more and more people enter the health care industry: planners, evaluators, advisers, purchasers, programmers, assistants to assistants to assistants. Of course, the salary for each must be absorbed by the patients, even though the patients themselves may never benefit one iota. The burgeoning care payroll has no correlation with the quality or quantity of patient care given.

There may be some similarities between your hospital and a nationally known laboratory that had the habit of plotting the growth of the organization graphically each year. Two graphs were used: one for the administrative staff and one for the scientific and technological staff. Soon it became obvious that administration had nearly tripled, whereas the number of scientists and technicians had remained almost constant. The solution was simple. Instead of cutting back on pencil pushers and red-tape worms or increasing the number of people actually doing the work, they simply opted to combine the graphs. Now the growth of the laboratory spirals ever upward, without making the proliferation of personnel parasites obvious.

A case in point may be one of the more recent positions to open up in the health care field: that of "patient advocate." First there was the token black, then the token woman, and now the token advocate. A lone individual, no matter how gifted or talented, cannot do what all of us who have vowed to serve and protect the patient cannot do. The existence of such a position provides false reassurance that the responsibility to stand up for the patient is no longer ours. "It's not my job, man. Let the advocate do it."

Much of the barnyard odor stems from the campaign to camouflage an inefficiently run industry as a charitable service. Health care is big business, and for women big business is still virtually off limits. To put business in a proper perspective, read *Up the Organization*,* the best-selling book by Robert Townsend. In very humorous, readable form, Townsend outlines business problems and solutions, many of which are applicable to the health professions today. He is daring, imaginative, irreverent, and thoroughly practical. If he could do for the health care industry what he did for Avis Rent-A-Car, being a professional or a patient would be more profitable and pleasurable.

If you are involved in management at any level, you will find his theories on people and work, including everything from memos to mistresses, not only entertaining but useful. Townsend is unorthodox enough to suggest abolishing whole departments, such as purchasing, personnel, and public relations. He calls job descriptions "straitjackets" and boldly proposes making everyone stand up through some meetings to make sure they are mercifully short.

Meetings are a trademark of bureaucratic barnyards. How many times have you left a meeting feeling good about what you have accomplished, and how many times have you left feeling that your time has been totally wasted?

---

*New York, 1970, Alfred A. Knopf, Inc.

Health professionals complain that they spend so much time in meetings talking about what should be done that there is no time left to do it.

If you share these feelings, check your calendar and appointment book. Are you attending meetings because *everyone* else does? Are you afraid of offending Big Daddy or Big Momma? Evaluate each meeting in light of the question: **Is what I am doing or about to do in the best interest of the patient?** Think of all the work that could be accomplished if *everyone* refused to attend meetings, refused to get bogged down in rhetoric, and finally admitted that hot air was getting us nowhere.

To further whet your appetite for Townsend's book, here is an entire chapter titled "Excellence: Or What the Hell Are You Doing Here?": "If you don't do it excellently, don't do it at all. Because if it's not excellent it won't be profitable or fun, and if you're not in business for fun or profit, what the hell are you doing here?"

Perhaps the time has come for you to ask yourself that question. What the hell are you doing in the health professions? If you work under conditions that do not permit you to do your work excellently, if the fun has gone out of your job, if it has not proved profitable for you or your patient, something is very wrong.

To right that wrong, you must first figure out what or who (self included) is keeping you from doing your work excellently. What obstacles stand between you and fun or profit?

If professionals do not receive satisfaction from their jobs, chances are neither will their patients. There are certain ingredients essential to job satisfaction. It does not matter whether a worker chooses to be a ditch digger, dietitian, bubble dancer, or doctor. Any worker's needs are basically these: belonging to a group, recognition, new experiences, and security.

Belonging to a group. Feelings of aloneness and isolation keep many women (especially housewives) from enjoying their jobs. No time to socialize and no one to socialize with are common complaints.

Within the health professions, work has become so specialized, so departmentalized and compartmentalized, that many of us feel a loneliness and isolation similar to that of housewives. Part-time workers and "floats" rarely feel they belong. Some express feeling like a visitor, an intruder, or a fifth wheel. Knowing that you are wanted, that you are welcome, that you belong is crucial to job satisfaction.

Even though your basic identity and strongest ties are wrapped up in family, you need a professional support group. You need colleagues with whom you can share both your joys and sorrows. You need people around you who understand and care about you and your work, people who share some of your experiences, dreams, fears, priorities, and goals.

Women still have a lot to learn about teamwork, camaraderie, fellowship, and esprit de corps. Anything you can do to foster a one-for-all-and-all-for-one feeling, to give yourself and your colleagues a sense of belonging, a strong sense of "our" unit (hospital, agency, clients), will increase job satisfaction.

Recognition. Women and women's work are often taken for granted. If you are hungry for recognition, most likely the women around you feel the same way. You may all feel uncared for, unappreciated, and unnoticed. How long has it been since you told someone, "Hey, I really like working with you!"

It is nice to get praise from high places—the head of the hospital, the chief surgeon, the director of nurses—but for now perhaps we should work on recognizing each other. Sincere compliments, acknowledgments of jobs well done, a simple "thank you" can work wonders when it comes to job satisfaction. Concrete phrases like "You are skillful with your hands" or "I admire the way you are able to organize your work" or "You certainly had a calming influence during that crisis" or "I feel confident when I have you as a team member."

Don't wait until a person retires or moves away to tell her how much she is appreciated. Every ego needs an occasional stroke for survival. That goes for doctors, head nurses, teachers, supervisors, and national leaders. If compliments were as quick and as bountiful as criticism, job satisfaction would increase immeasurably.

New experiences. For job satisfaction, it is essential to know the difference between specialization and stagnation. Everyone needs some variety, change, and challenge to keep growing. To shake things up, to keep awake and alert, try changing units, shifts, hospitals. Read! Attend a workshop. Take a class, even if it is in crochet. If you are community based, do a stint in the hospital; if hospital based, do a stint in the community.

There is no question that the health professions are demanding physically, mentally, and emotionally. Many of our jobs require great stamina and brute strength, since they involve bending, lifting, pulling, stretching, twisting, climbing, running, and being on our feet all day long. Add to the physical demands the emotional stress of being responsible for people who may be suffering or dying. Care, worry, sorrow, frustration, disappointment—all take their toll.

As you soak your feet, thankful just to have made it through another day, there is little energy left to reflect, plan, dream, or solve problems. Daily pressures, duties, and demands all crowd out the loftier, more noble goals you may have had when you first entered your profession.

Being ground-bound makes it difficult to get much perspective on the past, present, or future of the health care system. It makes it difficult to see beyond your own day-to-day work situation. You need some distance between yourself and the frenzied flock, a better vantage point from which to view problems and effect solutions.

One idea might be to work out an exchange program in which nurses, therapists, or social workers in the field change places with their counterparts in education every couple of years. Being on the front line would give educators an opportunity to get back to basics, to experience the problems encountered each day, and to try theories out in actual situations. Having workers move into the classroom would give students firsthand knowledge of life in the real world, with all its problems and pleasures. The workers could take some time to read, plan, and reflect before going back into practice.

When looking for new experiences, be sure to evaluate their relevance for you as an individual. Women health professionals have a history of feeling complimented when administration or medicine ordains us capable of absorbing some mundane task that they no longer desire to do. Women already do far more than our share of the world's menial tasks. Scut work seldom qualifies as a stimulating new experience.

Security. Certainly security involves salary, fringe benefits, and pension plans, but it includes much more. Security means some type of predictability in the job and its demands. It means having some control over our professional environment. "Social security" should be extended to include not being subject to the whims, tirades, or vindictiveness of others and not being desperate to please superiors. Security means having a sense of worth, confidence, and respect.

• • •

If you are not deriving much satisfaction from your job, perhaps you can see whether a problem of belonging, recognition, new experiences, or security is giving you the most difficulty. Do not be discouraged if you find your professional life lacking in all four areas. Just as you learned to tackle one turkey at a time, tackle one area at a time. Start small, and be persistent. Remember that assertiveness is goal oriented. You have to know what you want. As you perch atop the chicken coop, take time to assess where you've been, where you are, and where you would like to be.

Setting personal or professional goals is highly individual. To be a winner in life's game, you have to decide what "winning" is for you. Too many women are tempted to play by rules or for prizes that appeal to others. One woman's success is often another woman's failure.

Men and women have definite differences when it comes to defining "winners." It is fascinating to see how unsynchronized men's and women's needs and goals are at the same ages in life. If you thought growth and development stopped at age 18, read *Passages* by Gail Sheehy. Chapters such as

"Why Can't a Woman Be More Like a Man and a Man Be Less Like a Race-horse?" help explain, comfort, and encourage those of us who find we are still having growing pains in our middle and later years. As you approach asser-tiveness, it will make a difference whether you are in your 20's, 30's, 40's, or 50's. *Passages* will help women and men who are sick of barnyard mentality but afraid of heights to dare venture up to the mountaintop. The book may also help you avoid a trap that many women have fallen into—that of mimick-ing men.

Although it is true that men have it better than women in almost every sphere, being masculine in your desires, attitudes, or actions will not make you an optimum human being. It is as unhealthy and unproductive for women to adopt the male model as it is for women health professionals to adopt the medical model. Men's rules and men's prizes rarely have relevance for women. Under these circumstances, even women who are winners feel like losers.

Another trouble spot for men and women is the dependence-indepen-dence-interdependence spiral. It is supposed that each level represents one more step toward maturity. In our culture, however, men have been al-lowed—and encouraged—to occupy the independent level as their own. Women, who rarely taste independence, split their lives between the depen-dent and interdependent levels, resulting in a splitting headache.

We go from being dependent on our parents to being depended on by husbands and children. We are cared for and then suddenly jump to caring for others without ever really learning how to care for ourselves. It is almost as though women have missed a step and stumbled into maturity without recog-nizing it. Conflict and confusion arise because, although women may have arrived on the interdependent plateau in interpersonal relationships, we are still very dependent on men economically and politically. Our blatant de-pendence in these areas tends to obscure our interdependence in other areas.

Serving others is an interdependent function. However, those who are self-serving view it as a dependent function. Once again, it becomes critical to find a way of serving others without being subservient.

Much of the shame, anger, and unrest women are experiencing results from the mislabeling of our functions as dependent and the failure of both men and women to recognize these functions as interdependent. Although it is expedient for women to strive for more independence in economic and political situations, it would be disastrous for us to deny ourselves the social and emotional interdependence that we have already achieved.

Women have a working knowledge of interdependence. We understand and accept needing, feeling, giving, compromising, placing others first, shar-ing, and caring. We have firsthand knowledge of the cost in time and energy that is required to sustain and nurture other human beings. Yet each day, men who have far less experience and insight into these matters designate priorities and formulate policies that regulate birth, death, and everything in between.

Although it may be true that women do not know much about looking out for Number One, we know a great deal about looking out for others. If there is one area in which women excel, it is caregiving. This is why it is so unfortunate that women are excluded from the decision-making processes that regulate the who, what, when, where, why, and how of caregiving systems.

Watching congressional debates on abortion issues is a visual reminder of how women are excluded from decisions that uniquely and profoundly affect us. Although our elected officials may be able to legislate that a woman give life to a baby, they cannot legislate that she give love. Sadly, unwanted children too often grow up into unwanted adults. The eventual cost of nonabortions may really be staggering.

Although it is exhilarating to snatch a fetus or a felon from the jaws of death, that brief act sets years of caregiving in motion. The flash of medical or legal brilliance dims quickly, and the men move on to new conquests, while women move in to mop up. Over the years, women health professionals have spent much of their time caring for the living remains of legal and medical miracles. Men are too busy to salvage and sustain. Perhaps if they were required to share in these functions, they would come to the realization that death is not the worst thing that can happen to a human being.

But for now, salvaging and sustaining are women's work. Unless women in the health professions learn to speak up and stand up for the rights of humans, atrocities like the following will continue indefinitely.

Whatever happened to the Old West tradition of letting people die with their boots on? Today we won't even let them die with their feet on. On February 22, 1978, the Supreme Court rejected the pleas of 72-year-old Mary Northern of Nashville, Tennessee to prevent doctors from amputating her gangrenous feet. Lawyers for the "elderly recluse" said she had a "right to privacy" and a fundamental right of "bodily integrity." They observed that no lower court had ruled her incompetent for any purpose other than deciding· whether she needed this particular operation.

According to her lawyers, Mary had only a 5 to 10 percent chance of survival without the amputation and about a 50 percent chance of survival with it. Given only a fifty-fifty chance of survival, the will to live often tips the balance. A couple of years ago, a similar case received national attention. Another elderly woman had her leg amputated against her will. She died a few weeks after the operation.

If Mary Northern survives the surgery, what will her life be like? A woman who has lived alone for 17 years, suddenly denied her privacy, freedom, and independence. Consigned to a "businessing" or "doctoring" home or parking lot (formerly known as "nursing home") to await death. If you were forced to have such mutilating surgery against your will at the age of 72, how long do you think you would survive?

Perhaps it is not the function of physicians or state officials or Supreme Court justices to consider such things. But someone should consider such things. Perhaps the assertive thing for women in the health professions to do would be to form a humane society for humans. Dumb animals should not be the only ones protected from torture and mutilation.

Angels of mercy or accomplices to crime? You be the judge after reading about the following slice of life from the health care barnyard, vividly depicted in an article by Priscilla Johnson called "The Long, Hard Dying of Joe Rodriguez" (*American Journal of Nursing,* January 1977). She describes a nightmare situation involving a heroin addict who has been stabbed in the abdomen. He arrives on the intensive care unit from surgery still hemorrhaging, on a respirator, and with his entire pancreas and colon hopelessly necrotic. Not expected to live through the night, he manages to survive several days.

Joe is surrounded by machines, his body punctured with a dozen tubes. His care is laborious and mechanical. The physicians concentrate on tissues, organs, fluids, and electrolytes, apparently unable to see the forest for the trees.

A week after his admission, he hemorrhages, his gut falls out, and they race him to surgery doing CPR all the way. Somehow he survives surgery but is soon hemorrhaging again. The blood bank is screaming because it is bankrupt. The stench, the pain, the degradation, the futility are all explicitly detailed.

When the author leaves the room for a few minutes, she hears the angry reactions of women who question the terrible waste of blood, sweat, and tears. They plead to let him go. Everyone seems to agree what they are doing is wrong, everyone but the medical staff.

A new intern enters the case, telling the author that Joe's problem is reversible, that he can improve. Silently she questions: "Sir, do you really mean it? You're actually telling me that Joe will someday walk out of here—leaving his pancreas, his kidneys, his bowels behind? Is what they have told you true, or is it only that the insatiable vanity of the medical team will not admit defeat?"

Throughout the ordeal, the recurring question she asks herself is: "What is right, what is really loving Joe Rodriguez?" It is a question she does not ask aloud, because, as she says, "That question just doesn't seem to matter."

As she describes the situation, that question does not appear to matter to the medical staff, but it seems to matter a great deal to the nurses. Among themselves, they agonize over the standing order to resuscitate Joe Rodriguez. They question and cry, but they stop short of confronting the medical staff with their concerns and convictions.

Unfortunately, the Joe Rodriguez situation is not that uncommon. Most women in the health professions have a horror story or two to match this one. The time has come for women to loudly ask what is right, what is the loving thing to do. Women may be in a better position than men to assess whether life is being sustained or death is being prolonged.

Ostriches, get your heads out of the sand! These are only samples of the hard issues that need to be grappled with in the health professions, and they will not go away if ignored. The consequences of action or inaction are fearful. There are no simple solutions, no pat formulas for instant success. Assertiveness is not a cure-all. It is only a first step. But watch that first step; it's a long one.

Although the problems in health care may be bigger than both of us, they are not bigger than all of us. If women win the right to share equally with men in making life-and-death decisions, our rewards will be greater but so will our responsibilities. If you are too chicken to share those responsibilities, you had better begin again at page 1. If you are too tired or too timid to share the load, then pass your proxy to those who can. Let local and national leaders in political and professional organizations know where you stand on the tough issues.

The assertive response is basically to ask yourself: "What can *I* do? What can I do right *now?*" And then do it.

If there were a School of Assertiveness for Women in the Health Professions, this would be the school song:

LOOKING FOR SPACE*

John Denver

On the road of experience
I'm trying to find my own way
Sometimes I wish that I could fly away
When I think that I'm moving
Suddenly things stand still
I'm afraid 'cause I think they always will

  And I'm looking for space
  And to find out who I am

And I'm looking to know and
  understand
It's a sweet sweet dream
Sometimes I'm almost there
Sometimes I fly like an eagle and
Sometimes I'm deep in despair

All alone in the universe
Sometimes that's how it seems

I get lost in the sadness and the screams
Then I look in the center
Suddenly everything's clear
I find myself in the sunshine and my
dreams

    And I'm looking for space
    And to find out who I am
    And I'm looking to know and
      understand
    It's a sweet sweet dream
    Sometimes I'm almost there
    Sometimes I fly like an eagle and
    Sometimes I'm deep in despair

On the road of experience
Join in the living day
If there's an answer
It's just that it's just that way

    When you're looking for space
    And to find out who you are
    When you're looking to try and reach
      the stars
    It's a sweet sweet dream
    Sometimes I'm almost there
    Sometimes I fly like an eagle and
    Sometimes I'm deep in despair

Women are looking for space, for room in which to grow, to work, to live. There will be days when you will wish you had never heard of assertiveness, days when you wish you could just fly away and not have to toil in the health care barnyard. There will be days when you won't quite know who you are or what your place is. There will be days when things seem to stand still or, worse yet, days when you are sure things are moving backward. Take heart. These days are numbered.

On days when you feel all alone in the universe, get out and look for birds of a feather. Take the initiative to share some of what you are going through with others, and they may open up and share with you. Some may even dare join you if they know where you are going.

If you find yourself getting "lost in the sadness and the screams," keep your eye on the center—the patient. Focus on the patient, and you will be amazed at how the petty, peripheral things will float away, and your work will seem less complicated and cluttered.

Hunt and peck and scratch and claw, but take time to dream. Be prepared for some highs and lows, knowing that you are bound to win some and lose some. Know that nothing or no one is forever. Learn to let go of everything except your sense of humor.

Each reader will have to write her own epilogue. For now, here is a benediction:

> But they that wait upon the Lord shall renew their strength: they shall mount up with wings as eagles: they shall run, and not be weary: and they shall walk, and not faint. (Isaiah **40**:31)

Ready for lift-off? Then straighten up and fly . . . right?

Annotated bibliography

Adams, Linda, and Lenz, Elinor: Effectiveness training for women: E.T.W., 1979, Wyden Books.

Written by the wife of Thomas Gordon, author of *Parent Effectiveness Training* (P.E.T.), T.E.T. for teachers, and L.E.T. for leaders. This one is called "E.T.W.," probably for fear that if they called it "W.E.T." readers might suggest the book was all wet. Essentially a rehash of assertiveness training, it also includes a smattering of everything from problem solving to self-disclosure.

Alberti, Robert E., and Emmons, Michael L.: Your perfect right: A guide to assertive behavior, San Luis Obispo, Calif., 1970, Impact Series.

A pioneer effort in assertive training. Aims to enrich the humanity of all by increasing the self-esteem in each of us. Gives multiple case examples with conclusions to illustrate assertive, nonassertive, and aggressive behavior. Contains a step-by-step outline for asserting yourself, along with a guide to becoming a therapist and helping others become more assertive. Includes annotated bibliography.

Alberti, Robert E., and Emmons, Michael L.: Stand up, speak out, talk back! New York, 1975, Pocket Books.

After reading this book, many women feel they should have its title embossed on their T-shirts. Loaded with practical examples for social, school, and work situations. Contains tips on forming an assertive training group and on helping others learn to be assertive.

Baer, Jean: How to be an assertive (not aggressive) woman in life, in love, and on the job, New York, 1976, New American Library, Inc.

After a lifetime of "dependency training," the author encourages women to seek assertiveness training. Contains well-written, thoroughly documented, detailed case studies including interviews with several highly successful women. Tells how to spot your own blocks to assertiveness and gives exercises to overcome them. Emphasizes assertiveness in close relationships as well as on the job. Contains an entire chapter on children and assertiveness.

Billings, Victoria: The womansbook, Greenwich, Conn., 1974, Fawcett World Library.

Warm, witty, comforting, explanatory. Makes a crucial distinction between equality and independence and examines waiting as a life's work for women. Especially helpful for women trying to combine marriage, motherhood, and career. Indispensable reading for women who want to be "liberated" without having to abandon family life and loving relationships.

Bloom, Lynn Z., Coburn, Karen, and Pearlman, Joan: The new assertive woman, New York, 1976, Dell Publishing Co., Inc.

Helpful in understanding why women avoid assertiveness and how irrational fears about it may be overcome. Discusses games women play. Tells how to assess your own assertiveness or lack of it. Provides lots of examples and exercises for role-play situations. Encourages women who want to venture beyond the roles of wife and mother.

Campbell, David: If you don't know where you're going, you'll probably end up somewhere else, Niles, Ill., 1974, Argus Communications.

 The title is almost longer than the book. A concise, clever, creative discussion of the importance of making choices and setting goals instead of "stumbling across life." Useful for the young person selecting a career or for the person considering a midlife career change. And aren't we all?

Clark, Carolyn Chambers: Assertive skills for nurses, Wakefield, Mass., 1978, Nursing Resources, Inc.

 This how-to book is divided into learning modules for use by individuals or groups. Stuffed with exercises, situations, charts, scales, and other paper-and-pencil activities, it is bound to stimulate thinking. Good resource book for persons planning workshops or seminars.

Corea, Gena: The hidden malpractice, New York, 1977, Jove Publications, Inc.

 This carefully researched, well-written book traces the plight of women throughout history as they search for safe, sane health care. That search goes on today. Here is a chilling account of how the American medical system mistreats women—both as professionals and as patients. Man's ignorance of normal female functioning and consistent interference in normal processes such as childbirth have caused much death and destruction. A surprising amount of medical treatment of women is based on myths and misinformation that have no support or foundation in scientific fact. The author urges the demystification of medicine and the promotion of informed female health consumers. Read it and weep.

Ellis, Albert, and Knaus, William J.: Overcoming procrastination, New York, 1977, Signet.

 I haven't got around to reading this one yet.

Fensterheim, Herbert: Don't say yes when you want to say no, New York, 1975, Dell Publishing Co., Inc.

 Gives a strong theoretical background linking assertive training with behavior therapy. Includes an assertiveness inventory; instructions for setting goals and achieving them (for instance, how to get thin and stay thin); and suggestions for handling social situations, sexual relationships, habits, depression, and assertiveness on the job. Excellent case examples and some personal sharing by the author.

Harris, Thomas A.: I'm ok—you're ok: A practical guide to transactional analysis, New York, 1967, Harper & Row, Publishers.

 Excellent reading for those who want to explore TA in more detail. Clear presentation of the Parent, Adult, and Child in all of us. Gives practical situations and solutions for times when communication becomes snarled and tangled. Contains interesting chapters on moral values, social implications, and family interactions.

Hennig, Margaret, and Jardim, Anne: The managerial woman, New York, 1977, Pocket Books.

 Excellently written by two women with doctoral degrees from Harvard Business School. Although based on their work with women managers in the business world, the book has endless implications for working women everywhere. Intelligent, helpful view of the real world, not the ideal world. Explains differences between men and women regarding upbringing, expectations, opportunities, career choices, and constraints. Must reading for the professional woman seeking a career, not just a string of jobs.

Illich, Ivan: Medical nemesis, New York, 1976, Bantam Books, Inc.

 Indictment against the medical care system for causing as many sicknesses as it cures. Almost half the book is devoted to footnotes that expand or confirm the thought in the text. Fascinating and frightening. Urges people to reclaim their right to health by maintaining informed control of their own bodies.

Irish, Richard K.: If things don't improve soon I may ask you to fire me: The management book for everyone who works, Garden City, N.Y., 1975, Anchor Books.

If you have the responsibility for hiring and firing, this book is for you. Contains ample advice on how to recruit effective people and how to dismiss ineffective ones. For manager or worker, the emphasis is on defining what you want and the importance of taking risks. Distinguishes between growth jobs and dumb jobs, between head-hunting and herd-hunting.

Jongeward, Dorothy, and Scott, Dru: Women as winners: Transactional analysis for personal growth, Reading, Mass., 1979, Addison-Wesley Publishing Co., Inc.

A practical, positive book that draws on TA, Gestalt therapy, and life scripting to help women understand the past, survive the present, and succeed in the future. Explodes most of the myths and fairy tales women have unthinkingly embraced. Documents the harsh financial realities most women must face.

Jongeward, Dorothy, and Seyer, Philip: Choosing success: Transactional analysis on the job, New York, 1978, John Wiley & Sons, Inc.

For *STAT* readers interested in learning more about transactional analysis, this is an excellent book. The first half deals with TA on the job, and the second half focuses on one's personal life. Each chapter begins with objectives, ends with a summary, and is chock-full of examples, exercises, flowcharts, and illustrations. Whether you are a worker or a working supervisor, you will appreciate practical tips on such things as how to assertively disagree, how to manage your time, and how to confront people (subordinates, superiors, peers, and clients) in a straightforward manner.

Korda, Michael: Power! How to get it, how to use it, New York, 1975, Random House, Inc.

Depressing reading. One chapter is devoted to women and power, which basically explores women in the business world. In general, the author supports the well-known fact that when it comes to power, women don't have any.

Lair, Jess: I ain't much, baby—but I'm all I've got, Greenwich, Conn., 1969, Fawcett World Library.

While scrambling to become a millionaire at a job he hated, the 35-year-old author had a heart attack. He resolved "from this time on I am never again going to do something that I don't deeply believe in," and he completely altered his philosophy and life-style. The book is both inspirational and informative. Some chapters are "Accepting Yourself—Five Minutes at a Time" and "If There's a Problem Here—I Caused It." Deals with self-acceptance, change, love, courage, loss, and grief.

Miller, Jean Baker: Toward a new psychology of women, Boston, 1976, Beacon Press.

If women's subordinate position in society has ever made you furious or depressed, this book will explain, comfort, and challenge you. Based on clinical observations, the author examines conflict, cooperation, and creativity as well as other aspects of life. Dr. Miller sees within women strengths and insights that have been largely ignored. Invigorating glimpse into the future when both men and women can set aside rigid stereotypes and become fully human.

O'Reilly, Jane: The girl I left behind, New York, 1980, Macmillan Publishing Co., Inc.

Subtitled "The Housewife's Moment of Truth and Other Feminist Ravings," this book is a humorous, personal account of the people, places and events that made the author a feminist (a person—man or woman—who makes a conscious and continuous effort to improve the lives of all women). As a journalist O'Reilly discovered that the same problems face women all over the world: inadequate education, low wages, lack of political power, legal inequality, denial of control over their own bodies. Eventually, she discovered to her surprise that as a woman they were *her* problems too.

Ringer, Robert J.: Winning through intimidation, New York, 1973, Funk & Wagnalls, Inc.
Business-oriented success book that shoots down common theories of having a "positive mental attitude" and "working hard, long hours." Stresses acknowledging reality and using it to your benefit instead of trying to deal with a system in terms of what you wish it were or think it should be. Some keys to success are to be prepared, be good at necessary techniques, be goal oriented, be aware that life is short, and refuse to take yourself too seriously.

Rivers, Caryl, Barnett, Rosalind, and Baruch, Grace: Beyond sugar and spice: How women grow, learn, and thrive, New York, 1979, Ballantine Books, Inc.
Absolutely crammed with facts, figures, and personal and professional insights to help women understand their lives. If you have a daughter, this book will help you provide her with self-confidence, resourcefulness, and the general ability to take care of herself. Highly recommended.

Sheehy, Gail: Passages: Predictable crises of adult life, New York, 1974, E.P. Dutton & Co., Inc.
Must reading for any woman between the ages of 20 and 50. Most of us in the health professions have studied child growth and development. We have mistakenly concluded that this process ends with adolescence. It is reassuring and exciting to know that growth and change continue throughout life and that adult stages are as distinct, as fascinating, as painful, and as promising as any of the childhood stages. Especially helpful in understanding that men and women experience different stages at different ages.

Sheehy, Gail: Pathfinders, New York, 1981, William Morrow & Co., Inc.
If you relished *Passages*, you will delight in *Pathfinders* even more. Pathfinders are not charmed human beings but ordinary people from all age groups and all walks of life who have faced a crisis in an unusually creative way. The emphasis is on well-being, a state achieved by these people who were not afraid to take risks or make changes in their lives.

Smith, Manuel J.: When I say no, I feel guilty, New York, 1975, The Dial Press.
Extensive dialogues used to illustrate a variety of assertive techniques. Situations range from your bedroom to your place of business. If you are confused about what assertive speech sounds like, Smith offers abundant examples. He also provides a list of rights, including your right to say, "I don't care."

Taubman, Bryna: How to become an assertive woman, New York, 1976, Pocket Books.
Suggests that women should identify a life plan and then keep a daily log to see if the two are compatible. Takes a quick look at a multitude of common social situations best handled assertively. Discusses getting to know yourself, learning new roles and ways of coping, dealing with compliments and criticisms, and finding ways to express both anger and love. Quick reading. Helpful.

ISBN 0-8016-1135-0